CASE CLOSED

A Practical Guide to Mastering Pretrial Advocacy

ASPEN COURSEBOOK SERIES

CASE CLOSED

A Practical Guide to Mastering Pretrial Advocacy

VERONICA J. FINKELSTEIN
Associate Professor of Law
Wilmington University School of Law

KRISTIN L. WALKER
Professor of Practice and Faculty Director of Externships
Syracuse University College of Law

ASPEN PUBLISHING

Cover image credit: iStock.com/NanoStockk & iStock.com/Naypong

To contact Customer Service, e-mail customer.service@aspenpublishing.com, call 1-800-950-5259, or mail correspondence to:

Aspen Publishing
Attn: Order Department
1 Wall Street
Burlington, MA 01803

Printed in the United States of America.

1 2 3 4 5 6 7 8 9 0

ISBN 979-8-8941-0207-8

Library of Congress Cataloging-in-Publication Data

Names: Finkelstein, Veronica J., author. | Walker, Kristin L., author.
Title: Case closed : a practical guide to mastering pretrial advocacy/Veronica J. Finkelstein, Associate Professor of Law, Wilmington University School of Law; Kristin L. Walker, Professor of Practice and Faculty Director of Externships, Syracuse University College of Law.
Description: First edition. | Burlington : Aspen Publishing, 2025. | Includes index. | Summary: "Practical pretrial prep and exercises for law students" — Provided by publisher.
Identifiers: LCCN 2025020398 | ISBN 9798894102078 (paperback) | ISBN 9798894102108 (ebook)
Subjects: LCSH: Pre-trial procedure — United States.
Classification: LCC KF8900 .F56 2025 | DDC 347.73/72 — dc23/eng/20250429
LC record available at https://lccn.loc.gov/2025020398

ABOUT ASPEN PUBLISHING

Aspen Publishing is a leading provider of legal education content and digital learning solutions in the United States and globally. Our innovative products and platforms—designed based on best practices in learning science—engage students and enhance outcomes. From textbooks and audiobooks authored by renowned experts to digital platforms and products like LEAF, Connected eBooks, Connected Quizzing, PracticePerfect, and JD-Next, we empower the next generation of legal professionals with innovative, trusted, and accessible resources.

The Aspen Casebook Series, affectionately known as the "red and black" casebooks among law faculty and students, includes hundreds of highly regarded textbooks across more than 80 disciplines. These range from foundational courses like Torts and Contracts to emerging electives such as Sustainability and the Law of Policing. Our study aids, including the popular *Examples & Explanations* series, help law students master complex topics with clarity and confidence.

Aspen's expertise extends to undergraduate education with our Paralegal, Criminal Justice, and Business Law series, offering the same hallmark quality to a broader audience. JD-Next, our groundbreaking online law school prep course and admissions test, provides a realistic preview of law school, equips students with essential skills for academic success, and evaluates their readiness for legal studies.

Aspen Publishing Is Proud to Be a UWorld Company

Since 2003, UWorld has been a global leader in developing high-quality learning tools for students preparing for high-stakes exams. With a commitment to excellence, UWorld has helped millions of students in undergraduate, graduate, and professional programs in fields such as medicine, nursing, finance, and law achieve their academic and career goals.

Founded by Chandra S. Pemmasani, M.D., during his medical residency, UWorld began focusing on medical education and has since expanded into various academic fields, including law. In 2020, UWorld launched its Legal vertical, starting with its comprehensive Multistate Bar Exam (MBE®) Question Bank, followed by the acquisition of Themis Bar Review, which integrated resources to provide a complete bar exam preparation experience. In 2024, UWorld expanded its offerings by acquiring Aspen Publishing, enhancing its suite of legal education products.

Today, UWorld offers an unparalleled range of study materials that blend active learning methods with expert content, ensuring students and educators can access the most effective resources. From bar preparation to law school success, UWorld is committed to supporting the next generation of legal professionals. Learn more at uworld.com.

To Joseph Cohn, whose patience and confidence enabled me to pursue my dream of full time teaching (and everything that accompanies, including publishing).

-VJF

To my most prized professional mentors, the most inspiring of whom is my father; and to my mother, for encouraging me to write.

-KLW

CONTENTS

ABOUT THE AUTHORS

Veronica J. Finkelstein is an accomplished litigator, professor, and legal scholar whose career has been defined by her dedication to the law, both in the courtroom and the classroom. With a distinguished background in trial and appellate advocacy, she has handled high-stakes litigation for the federal government while also helping to develop the next generation of legal professionals.

As a litigator, Finkelstein served as an Assistant United States Attorney for over a decade, where she was recognized for her outstanding trial skills and ability to handle complex civil litigation. In her role as Senior Litigation Counsel, she was responsible for training and mentoring attorneys while managing high-profile fraud, employment discrimination, and medical malpractice cases on behalf of the federal government. Her litigation successes include securing winning verdicts in multiple jury and bench trials, negotiating multimillion-dollar settlements in healthcare and procurement fraud cases, and successfully arguing appeals. Finkelstein's ability to combine legal acumen with strategic advocacy earned her numerous accolades, including the Executive Office of United States Attorneys Director's Award for Superior Performance as a Civil Assistant United States Attorney and recognition from the Office of the Inspector General.

Beyond the courtroom, Finkelstein has devoted her career to legal education. She currently serves as an Associate Professor of Law at Wilmington University School of Law. Prior to her tenure at Wilmington University, she was a Practice Professor of Law at Drexel University's Thomas R. Kline School of Law and has held adjunct positions at Emory University School of Law and Rutgers Law School. Her teaching portfolio spans trial advocacy, appellate advocacy, evidence, pretrial litigation, professional responsibility, and legal writing. As a longtime faculty advisor and coach of moot court and mock trial teams, she has played a pivotal role in shaping students into skilled advocates.

Finkelstein has also distinguished herself as an exceptional instructor of National Institute for Trial Advocacy (NITA) programs. She has trained attorneys in deposition skills, motion practice, and trial advocacy. She frequently donates her time teaching in NITA's public interest programs and was selected as the 2025 recipient of NITA's Jo Ann Harris Public Service Award.

Kristin L. Walker is a full-time Professor of Practice and serves as the Faculty Director of Externships at Syracuse University College of Law. A practitioner by background, Kristin brings the nuances of practice into the classroom, teaching a spectrum of courses, including first-year Legal Communication and Research, upper-level Transactional Drafting classes, and pretrial practice skills and theory in an experiential Advanced Litigation Skills course. Kristin teaches students across both the College's JD Residential and JD Interactive programs. Additionally, as Faculty Director of Externships for the College of Law, Kristin conducts live seminar courses which accompany each student's externship placement and created asynchronous classes as part of the mixed-format program.

Prior to joining the faculty, Professor Walker was a full-time practitioner at firms in both New York City and Syracuse, having gained years of experience in both corporate and litigation practice areas. Notably, she began her law career with the law firm of McCarter & English LLP, where she practiced in the firm's Corporate, Securities, and Financial Institutions practice group in New York City. Transitioning to upstate New York, Kristin expanded her practice to include litigation experience, in both defense and plaintiff's capacities. Kristin credits her expansive practical experience with imparting the depth and breadth of material to share with students as they learn the practical application of foundational concepts and theory.

Kristin Walker graduated cum laude from Syracuse University College of Law in 2008 where she served as Managing Editor of the Syracuse Law Review from 2007 to 2008. While in law school, she clerked for Judge David N. Hurd of the U.S. District Court for the Northern District of New York and interned at the U.S. District Attorney's Office. She received her B.A., magna cum laude, from Villanova University in 2002. Kristin is admitted to practice law in New York and New Jersey.

ACKNOWLEDGMENTS

The authors gratefully acknowledge the permission granted to reprint works from the following copyright holders:

Nigh, Ty. "Manchester Town Hall Extension and Central Library." Photograph. Flickr via Wikimedia Commons, https://commons.wikimedia.org/wiki/File:USPS_Truck_(53417022474).jpg. Licensed under CC BY 2.0. https://creativecommons.org/licenses/by/2.0/.

PART I

INTRODUCTION

You probably read judicial opinions in many of your law school classes, including in your civil procedure course. These opinions required the judge to apply procedural rules at various stages of the litigation process. Reading them helped you understand black letter law, but they probably left you with more questions than answers about the litigation process itself.

Perhaps you read *Matos v. Nextran, Inc.* in your civil procedure class. In that case, the plaintiff Eduardo Matos was driving a truck carrying concrete which rolled over and badly injured him. The truck, which was owned by the plaintiff's employer, was allegedly manufactured and sold by defendant Nextran. Plaintiff's complaint contained a variety of claims, including one against Nextran for violation of an express warranty. Nextran moved to dismiss this and other claims under Federal Rule of Civil Procedure 12(b)(6).

In deciding the motion, the United States Supreme Court had to evaluate the Rule 12(b)(6) standard. Ultimately, it decided that although the complaint lacked necessary facts about any warranty, the complaint should be dismissed without prejudice to allow plaintiff an opportunity to gather additional facts and plead them in a subsequent amended complaint.

Reading this case certainly helped you understand Rule 12(b)(6). But reading this case didn't reveal all the work behind the scenes that culminated in the opinion. Nor did it show you what happened next.

Indeed, the opinions that fill law school textbooks are helpful for learning the law, but that's not why those opinions were written. Those opinions were issued by judges handling real disputes between actual parties. These opinions arose because of, and in the context of, litigation.

Think about *Matos v. Nextran, Inc.* Many things had to happen before the judge could apply Rule 12(b)(6) to the complaint. The plaintiff had to retain a lawyer. That lawyer had to do some preliminary fact gathering. Then the lawyer had to draft and file the complaint. Think about what happened after the opinion was issued. Plaintiff's counsel was given an opportunity to amend the complaint. Before doing so, the lawyer would need to gather additional facts. What tools did the lawyer have to gather these facts? These are all issues your casebook didn't address.

You probably also read *Celotex Corp. v. Catrett* in your civil procedure class. In that case, the plaintiff, Myrtle Nell Catrett, sued Celotex Corporation for wrongful death, alleging that her husband had been exposed to Celotex products containing asbestos, which led to his death. Celotex moved for summary judgment, arguing that Catrett had failed to produce sufficient evidence showing that her husband was exposed to Celotex's products. In response, Catrett provided three documents, including a deposition and letters, to show her husband had been exposed to products containing asbestos. She had no evidence, however, suggesting who manufactured these products.

In deciding the motion, the Supreme Court had to evaluate the Federal Rule of Civil Procedure 56 standard to determine whether the plaintiff met her burden. The Court determined that a party moving for summary judgment does not need to provide affirmative evidence negating the opponent's claim but can simply point out a lack of evidence. This case clarified the burden on the moving party under Rule 56.

Reading this case certainly helped you understand Rule 56. But reading this case didn't explain how the parties found themselves in a posture where they were able to move for summary judgment. The parties had to exchange information through a process known as discovery. Among that information were the letters attached to the plaintiff's opposition. The deposition transcripts were also created through this process. The plaintiff, through her counsel, had taken a deposition — a live, recorded question-and-answer-session where testimony was elicited. Reading the case might hint at the importance of civil discovery, but it did little to explain how that discovery process actually unfolds. Your civil procedure casebook didn't teach you how to request documents under Federal Rule of Civil Procedure 34 or how to properly notice and take a deposition under Rule 30.

Our goal with this book is not only to concisely answer these and many other questions you may have about the civil litigation process but also to provide an opportunity for you to develop the sorts of practical skills you'll need to be a successful litigator yourself. We want you to be able to step into the kinds of situations presented in *Matos v. Nextran, Inc.* and *Celotex Corp. v. Catrett* and not only understand the procedural rules but understand how to use them as a powerful tool to advocate for a client.

Using this book, you will learn about civil litigation and develop skills in the context of a realistic personal injury case file arising from a car accident. As you will learn, the accident occurred on November 10, Y-2.[1] On that date, there was a collision at the intersection of Route 38 and Larchmont Boulevard

1. This book express dates in relation to the current date. Y-1 means the current year, minus one. So, if the current year is 2025, events occurring in Y-1 occurred in 2024, events occurring in Y-2 occurred in 2023, etc. You should substitute the actual year for the relation to the current year expression of the dates provided in the book.

in Wildcat City between a United States Postal Service (USPS) truck, driven by Postal Service employee Riley Royal, and a car driven by Skylar Schott. Royal and Schott disagree about who was at fault for the collision. Neither driver had a passenger and there were no eyewitnesses, but Wildcat Police Officer Pat Swalsky arrived at the scene soon after the collision. After the accident, Schott sought medical treatment from primary care physician Sydney David. Royal was uninjured.

Any claims for personal injury in this dispute are governed by the Federal Tort Claims Act (FTCA). Under the FTCA, the federal government can be held liable for the negligent or wrongful acts or omissions of its employees acting within the scope of their official duties. The only proper defendant under the FTCA is the United States, not the federal employee or the agency that employed that individual.

A person wishing to make a claim for reimbursement under the FTCA must first file an administrative claim with the appropriate federal agency. The agency, therefore, has an opportunity to investigate the claim and resolve it prior to any litigation. Here, Schott tendered an administrative claim to the USPS (before retaining you or your classmates as counsel), but the dispute was not resolved administratively. It now appears that civil litigation will be necessary between Schott and the United States.

When using this book, you should put yourself in the shoes of the attorney representing either Schott or the United States. It will be your responsibility to litigate this case on behalf of your client through the pleadings, discovery, and pre-trial phases of the case. To do so, you will need to put everything you have learned about civil procedure into action.

Because this case will be litigated in federal court, you should assume the Federal Rules of Civil Procedure apply. Although this book will contain much of the material you will need to fully litigate the case, at times you will be provided with other information and instructions from your professor. Litigating a case from start to finish may feel like a daunting task, but this book will provide you with all the guidance you need along the way.

Let's get started!

HOW TO USE THIS BOOK

Law schools are increasingly teaching practical skills. This shift is beneficial to students like you. Learning practical skills in law school will give you both the confidence and competence you need to succeed in practice. Practicing these skills in a simulated setting should prepare you to hit the ground running in your career.

Learning these skills now will not only prepare you for practice, but they'll also give you an edge on passing the bar exam. The NextGen Bar Exam is scheduled to debut in July 2026, eventually replacing the Uniform Bar Examination. The NextGen Bar Exam will test a range of lawyering skills, including legal research, writing, and negotiation. It will be fully integrated and scenario-based, asking you to perform tasks in a realistic case file.

It's clear that practical skills are important for your success. But how will you learn those skills? That's where this book comes in.

This book is not like most of the books you've used in law school. It's not full of reported cases. Nor does it contain long-form, narrative chapters. Instead, it presents you with a realistic case file followed by a series of brief explanations and exercises. It is designed to give you the experience of working on a tort case from start to finish, learning necessary litigation skills along the way.

The book is organized into two main parts. Part II is the case file itself. You should start by reading and familiarizing yourself with this material. As in the case of actual litigation, the case will develop over time. You have material to begin with, and you will learn additional information during the course of the litigation that will change and supplement this initial information — but it's what you have now, to start. Part of your task in learning to litigate will be developing a system to organize and structure your thoughts about the case. For now, read the case file as though you are a neutral detective trying to determine what happened and why. Later, you'll switch to advocacy mode after you've been assigned to represent one party in the litigation.

Part III contains a series of explanations and exercises. Each puts you in the role of an advocate for one of the parties in this case. With a few exceptions, exercises are to be completed by both plaintiff's counsel and defense counsel. There is a notation for the few exercises exclusive to one side of the case. These exercises put you in the position of actively litigating the case. They call on you to perform a skill or skills. Sometimes the work product will be written; other times you will prepare for a simulation.

We want you to go into the exercise feeling prepared to execute that skill. For this reason, each exercise is preceded by an explanation. The explanations are meant to supplement, rather than replace, what you learn in class or from other assigned readings. They are meant to orient you to each assignment, assuming you have a basic understanding of civil procedure and torts and simply need some pointers about how to apply that understanding to a specific stage of litigation. Your professor may not assign all of the exercises and may choose to have you submit written work products, engage in a simulation, or both. Even where an exercise has not been assigned, you may find it helpful to read the provided explanation and envision how you might have performed the exercise prior to moving on to the next stage of litigation. Each exercise provides instructions, so you know exactly what tasks you need to complete to advance the ball on litigating your case.

We have designed this book, including the case file, to be realistic, easy-to-use, flexible, and practical. We hope it will let you truly develop necessary litigation skills through active participation rather than passive reading. However you use it, we hope you enjoy the process.

PART II

ADMINISTRATIVE CASE FILE

Chief Counsel, Torts
General Law Service Center
USPS National Tort Center
1720 Market Street, Room 2400
St. Louis, MO 63155-9948

February 26, Y-0

To Whom it May Concern:

I write seeking damages of $100,000 as a result of a car accident on November 10, Y-2. Enclosed, please find:

- A completed SF-95;
- The Wildcat City Police Department report for the accident;
- Photographs of my car showing the damage from the accident;
- The In'N'Out Auto Repair bill for repairing the damage; and
- The medical record from my evaluation in the emergency room on the day of the accident.

Please let me know if you need anything further. I look forward to your prompt response.

Sincerely,

Skylar Schott

CLAIM FOR DAMAGE, INJURY, OR DEATH	INSTRUCTIONS: Please read carefully the instructions on the reverse side and supply information requested on both sides of this form. Use additional sheet(s) if necessary. See reverse side for additional instructions.	FORM APPROVED OMB NO. 1105-0008

1. Submit to Appropriate Federal Agency:	2. Name, address of claimant, and claimant's personal representative if any. (See instructions on reverse). Number, Street, City, State and Zip code.
United States Postal Service	Skylar Schott

3. TYPE OF EMPLOYMENT	4. DATE OF BIRTH	5. MARITAL STATUS	6. DATE AND DAY OF ACCIDENT	7. TIME (A.M. OR P.M.)
☐ MILITARY ☒ CIVILIAN	07/11/Y-45	Married	Nov. 10 Y-2	9:30am

8. BASIS OF CLAIM (State in detail the known facts and circumstances attending the damage, injury, or death, identifying persons and property involved, the place of occurrence and the cause thereof. Use additional pages if necessary).

I was injured in a car accident caused by the inattentive driving of USPS mail carrier Riley Royal. The accident happened on 11/10/Y-2 at approximately 9:30am at the intersection of Route 38 and Larchmont Blvd. in Wildcat City. Royal made a turn without signaling, cutting in front of me. Despite the fact that I swerved to avoid the USPS truck as much as I could, the front of my car impacted the back of the USPS truck. I suffered a concussion (with ongoing migraines) as well as neck/spine injuries as a result of the accident. My car was also damaged and had to be repaired.

9. PROPERTY DAMAGE

NAME AND ADDRESS OF OWNER, IF OTHER THAN CLAIMANT (Number, Street, City, State, and Zip Code).

N/A

BRIEFLY DESCRIBE THE PROPERTY, NATURE AND EXTENT OF THE DAMAGE AND THE LOCATION OF WHERE THE PROPERTY MAY BE INSPECTED. (See instructions on reverse side).

Damage to the front passenger side of my car, has been repaired, bills and photographs provided

10. PERSONAL INJURY/WRONGFUL DEATH

STATE THE NATURE AND EXTENT OF EACH INJURY OR CAUSE OF DEATH, WHICH FORMS THE BASIS OF THE CLAIM. IF OTHER THAN CLAIMANT, STATE THE NAME OF THE INJURED PERSON OR DECEDENT.

Concussion
Migraines
Neck strain/sprain
Back strain/spain

11. WITNESSES

NAME	ADDRESS (Number, Street, City, State, and Zip Code)
N/A	N/A

12. (See instructions on reverse). AMOUNT OF CLAIM (in dollars)

12a. PROPERTY DAMAGE	12b. PERSONAL INJURY	12c. WRONGFUL DEATH	12d. TOTAL (Failure to specify may cause forfeiture of your rights).
10,000.00	90,000.00	0.00	100,000.00

I CERTIFY THAT THE AMOUNT OF CLAIM COVERS ONLY DAMAGES AND INJURIES CAUSED BY THE INCIDENT ABOVE AND AGREE TO ACCEPT SAID AMOUNT IN FULL SATISFACTION AND FINAL SETTLEMENT OF THIS CLAIM.

13a. SIGNATURE OF CLAIMANT (See instructions on reverse side).	13b. PHONE NUMBER OF PERSON SIGNING FORM	14. DATE OF SIGNATURE
Skylar Schott	(555) 123-4567	Feb. 26, Y-2

CIVIL PENALTY FOR PRESENTING FRAUDULENT CLAIM	CRIMINAL PENALTY FOR PRESENTING FRAUDULENT CLAIM OR MAKING FALSE STATEMENTS
The claimant is liable to the United States Government for a civil penalty of not less than $5,000 and not more than $10,000, plus 3 times the amount of damages sustained by the Government. (See 31 U.S.C. 3729).	Fine, imprisonment, or both. (See 18 U.S.C. 287, 1001.)

Authorized for Local Reproduction
Previous Edition is not Usable
95-109

NSN 7540-00-634-4046

STANDARD FORM 95 (REV. 2/2007)
PRESCRIBED BY DEPT. OF JUSTICE
28 CFR 14.2

INSURANCE COVERAGE

In order that subrogation claims may be adjudicated, it is essential that the claimant provide the following information regarding the insurance coverage of the vehicle or property.

15. Do you carry accident insurance? ☐ Yes If yes, give name and address of insurance company (Number, Street, City, State, and Zip Code) and policy number. ☒ No

16. Have you filed a claim with your insurance carrier in this instance, and if so, is it full coverage or deductible? ☐ Yes ☒ No

17. If deductible, state amount.

18. If a claim has been filed with your carrier, what action has your insurer taken or proposed to take with reference to your claim? (It is necessary that you ascertain these facts).
N/A

19. Do you carry public liability and property damage insurance? ☐ Yes If yes, give name and address of insurance carrier (Number, Street, City, State, and Zip Code). ☒ No

INSTRUCTIONS

Claims presented under the Federal Tort Claims Act should be submitted directly to the "appropriate Federal agency" whose employee(s) was involved in the incident. If the incident involves more than one claimant, each claimant should submit a separate claim form.

Complete all items - Insert the word NONE where applicable.

A CLAIM SHALL BE DEEMED TO HAVE BEEN PRESENTED WHEN A FEDERAL AGENCY RECEIVES FROM A CLAIMANT, HIS DULY AUTHORIZED AGENT, OR LEGAL REPRESENTATIVE, AN EXECUTED STANDARD FORM 95 OR OTHER WRITTEN NOTIFICATION OF AN INCIDENT, ACCOMPANIED BY A CLAIM FOR MONEY DAMAGES IN A **SUM CERTAIN** FOR INJURY TO OR LOSS OF PROPERTY, PERSONAL INJURY, OR DEATH ALLEGED TO HAVE OCCURRED BY REASON OF THE INCIDENT. THE CLAIM MUST BE PRESENTED TO THE APPROPRIATE FEDERAL AGENCY WITHIN **TWO YEARS** AFTER THE CLAIM ACCRUES.

Failure to completely execute this form or to supply the requested material within two years from the date the claim accrued may render your claim invalid. A claim is deemed presented when it is received by the appropriate agency, not when it is mailed.

If instruction is needed in completing this form, the agency listed in item #1 on the reverse side may be contacted. Complete regulations pertaining to claims asserted under the Federal Tort Claims Act can be found in Title 28, Code of Federal Regulations, Part 14. Many agencies have published supplementing regulations. If more than one agency is involved, please state each agency.

The claim may be filed by a duly authorized agent or other legal representative, provided evidence satisfactory to the Government is submitted with the claim establishing express authority to act for the claimant. A claim presented by an agent or legal representative must be presented in the name of the claimant. If the claim is signed by the agent or legal representative, it must show the title or legal capacity of the person signing and be accompanied by evidence of his/her authority to present a claim on behalf of the claimant as agent, executor, administrator, parent, guardian or other representative.

If claimant intends to file for both personal injury and property damage, the amount for each must be shown in item number 12 of this form.

The amount claimed should be substantiated by competent evidence as follows:

(a) In support of the claim for personal injury or death, the claimant should submit a written report by the attending physician, showing the nature and extent of the injury, the nature and extent of treatment, the degree of permanent disability, if any, the prognosis, and the period of hospitalization, or incapacitation, attaching itemized bills for medical, hospital, or burial expenses actually incurred.

(b) In support of claims for damage to property, which has been or can be economically repaired, the claimant should submit at least two itemized signed statements or estimates by reliable, disinterested concerns, or, if payment has been made, the itemized signed receipts evidencing payment.

(c) In support of claims for damage to property which is not economically repairable, or if the property is lost or destroyed, the claimant should submit statements as to the original cost of the property, the date of purchase, and the value of the property, both before and after the accident. Such statements should be by disinterested competent persons, preferably reputable dealers or officials familiar with the type of property damaged, or by two or more competitive bidders, and should be certified as being just and correct.

(d) **Failure to specify a sum certain will render your claim invalid and may result in forfeiture of your rights.**

PRIVACY ACT NOTICE

This Notice is provided in accordance with the Privacy Act, 5 U.S.C. 552a(e)(3), and concerns the information requested in the letter to which this Notice is attached.

A. *Authority:* The requested information is solicited pursuant to one or more of the following: 5 U.S.C. 301, 28 U.S.C. 501 et seq., 28 U.S.C. 2671 et seq., 28 C.F.R. Part 14.

B. *Principal Purpose:* The information requested is to be used in evaluating claims.

C. *Routine Use:* See the Notices of Systems of Records for the agency to whom you are submitting this form for this information.

D. *Effect of Failure to Respond:* Disclosure is voluntary. However, failure to supply the requested information or to execute the form may render your claim "invalid."

PAPERWORK REDUCTION ACT NOTICE

This notice is solely for the purpose of the Paperwork Reduction Act, 44 U.S.C. 3501. Public reporting burden for this collection of information is estimated to average 6 hours per response, including the time for reviewing instructions, searching existing data sources, gathering and maintaining the data needed, and completing and reviewing the collection of information. Send comments regarding this burden estimate or any other aspect of this collection of information, including suggestions for reducing this burden, to the Director, Torts Branch, Attention: Paperwork Reduction Staff, Civil Division, U.S. Department of Justice, Washington, DC 20530 or to the Office of Management and Budget. Do not mail completed form(s) to these addresses.

STANDARD FORM 95 REV. (2/2007) **BACK**

WILDCAT POLICE DEPARTMENT

POLICE REPORT

Case Number: 2251 — Date: November 10, Y-2

Reporting Officer: Pat Swalsky — Report Prepared By: Pat Swalsky

Crash Date: November 10, YR-2 — Crash Time: 9:30 A.M. — Fatality: No

Location of Crash: Intersection of Route 38 and Larchmont Boulevard, Wildcat City

Unit Description (Unit 1)					
Make:	Honda	Model:	CRV	LP No.:	AAA555
Color:	Gray	Damage:	Front Passenger		
Driver:	Skylar Schott	DL No.:	123ABC456		
Passenger:	None				
Unit Description (Unit 2)					
Make:	Grumman	Model:	LLV	LP No.:	BBB111
Color:	White	Damage:	Minor, throughout		
Driver:	Riley Royal	DL No.:	789DEF123		
Passenger:	None				

Investigator's Narrative	Field Diagram (not to scale)
Dispatched to the intersection of Route 38 and Larchmont Boulevard in Wildcat City around 9:30 A.M. on November 10, YR-2. Arrived to the scene around 9:45 A.M. Upon arrival, approached Unit 1, which was parked on the side of the road on Route 38 facing North. Interviewed the driver, Skylar Schott. Schott described the crash as follows:	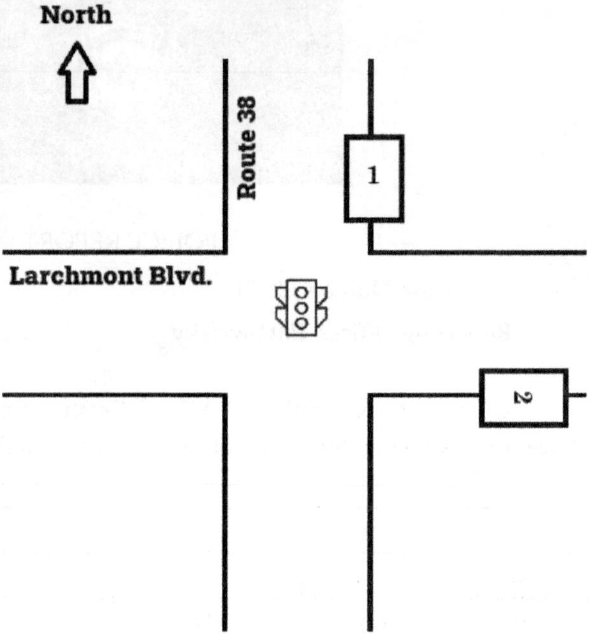

"I was driving on Route 38, heading towards the intersection with Larchmont. Coming the oppose direction was a white postal truck. I noticed it was weaving in the lane. Without putting on a turn signal, the truck suddenly made a right turn, cutting in front of me, onto Larchmont. I would have T-boned the truck, but at the last minute I swerved to the left. The front of my car clipped the back of the truck's bumper, and I was jolted to the side. I don't know if I hit my head or blacked out.

Once I realized what had happened, I pulled my car over to the side of Route 38. Some time passed, I'm not sure how long. The driver of the truck came over and asked if I was okay. I didn't know what to do, so I didn't say anything. I've just been waiting for you to get here."

Inquired as to whether Schott wanted me to call an ambulance. Schott declined.

Inspected Unit 1. Noted extensive damage to the front passenger side of the vehicle, consistent with a collision between that vehicle and another. No airbags deployed.

Approached Unit 2, which was parked on the side of the road on Larchmont Boulevard facing east.

Interviewed the driver, Riley Royal. Royal described the crash as follows:

"I was driving on Route 38, planning to turn left on Larchmont. As I neared the intersection, I put on my turn signal. There were no cars coming, so I began to turn. As I did, a car came flying up Route 38 going really fast. The car tried to get through the intersection as I was finishing my turn. It swerved around me, but didn't entirely miss the back of my truck. I felt a bump, so I know the car hit the back end of the truck.

I immediately pulled over and went to see if the other driver was okay. The driver was on the phone with someone and refused to roll the window down or talk to me. I asked whether the police had been called, but didn't get a response. So, I called 911 to report the accident. Then I went back to the truck to wait."

Inquired as to whether Royal wanted me to call an ambulance. Royal declined.

Inspected Unit 2. No major damage noted, minor damage throughout. No airbags deployed.

Inspected the intersection. No visible tire tracks. Traffic signals appeared to be in working order.

Unable to determine fault. No citation issued.

Left the scene around 10:20 A.M.

Pat Swalsky 11/10/Y-2

IN'N'OUT AUTO REPAIR
Your choice for fast and reliable service

BODY SHOP INVOICE

DATE IN: 11/13/Y-2
TIME IN: 11:30am
INVOICE #: 1790

Customer: Skylar Schott

PLATE	YEAR	MAKE	MODEL	COLOR
AAA555	2020	Honda	CRV	Gray

SERVICE DESCRIPTION	HOURS	RATE ($/HR)	TOTAL
Front end repair (accident)	60	$125	$7,500
-Frame repair			
-Align suspension			
-Bumper, front end panel, and light repair			
		TOTAL LABOR	

MATERIALS / PARTS DESCRIPTION	QUANTITY	COST	TOTAL
Bumper	1	$350	$350
Lights	1	$400	$400
Paint	n/a	$1,500	$1,500
		TOTAL PARTS	$2,250
		SUBTOTAL	
		DISCOUNT	
		TAX	
		TOTAL	$9,750

NOTES / CUSTOMER REQUESTS:
Uninsured motorist

THANK YOU FOR YOUR BUSINESS

UNIVERSITY OF WILDCAT HOSPITAL EMERGENCY DEPARTMENT □ Mass Casualty

Form to be used with WHO Reference Card. See who.int/emergencycare for more information.

Hospital Registration Number: 19811	Date: 11/10/Y-2	Time of Arrival: 11 : 00 (24h)

Patient Surname: Skylar First Name:	Age: 45 INF / CH / AD	Arrival Mode: □Ambulance □Car/Truck (*circle* Private or Taxi) □ Motorized 2/3-wheeler (*circle* Private or Taxi) □ Public Transport □ Walk □ Other: ________
Gender: □Male □Female □ Other: ________ / Date of Birth: 7/11/Y-45	Weight: kg	Number of prior facilities: ___ Referred from:
Occupation: Retail sales □ Unknown Patient Residence (at least City and Sub-district): 55 Main Street, Wildcat City □ Unknown		Sub-district where injury occurred: Wildcat City □ Unknown
Contact Person: Casey Schott	Phone: (555) 543-1212	Relation: Spouse

CHIEF COMPLAINT: Neck pain **Triage Category:** Low

INITIAL VS at 11 : 12 (24h) RR: 15 SpO_2: 98 % on room
Temp: 99.0 BP: 97 / 70 Pulse: 72 bpm Pain score (see Ref Card for details): 6 / 10 □ **Dead on arrival**

TREATING PROVIDER ASSESSMENT: Date: 11/10/Y-2 **Time:** 11: 53 (24h)

PRIMARY SURVEY (see Reference Card for normal findings, only mark NML if all key elements are normal):

Airway □ NML	□ Angioedema □ Stridor □ Voice changes □ Oral/Airway burns **Obstructed by:** □ Tongue □ Blood □ Secretions □ Vomit □ Foreign body	**Airway:** □ Repositioning □ Suction □ OPA □ NPA □ LMA □ BVM □ ETT **Spine stabilized:** □ Not needed □ Done before arrival □ Done in EU (not needed = not altered, no pain or TTP, no distracting injury, no focal neuro deficit)
Breathing □ NML	**Spontaneous Respiratory Rate:** ________ **Chest Rise:** □ Shallow □ Retractions □ Paradoxical **Trachea:** □ Midline □Deviated to □L □R **Breath Sounds:** □ L________ □ R________	**Oxygen:** ____ L □NC □Mask □NRB □BVM □CPAP/BIPAP □Ventilator: ________ **Chest needle / tube** (circle): □ L – Size: ____ Depth: ____ cm □ R – Size: ____ Depth: ____ cm □ **3-sided dressing**
Circulation □ NML	**Skin:** □ Warm □ Dry □ Pale □ Cyanotic □ Moist □ Cool **Capillary refill:** □ <3 sec or ____ sec **Pulses:** □ Weak □ Asymmetric____ **JVD:** □ Yes □No	□ Bleeding controlled (bandage, tourniquet, direct pressure) **Access:** □IV: Loc ________ Size ____ □CVL: Loc ____ Size ____ □IO: Loc ____ Size ____ □**IVF:** ________mLs □NS □LR □Other________ □Blood ordered □Pelvis stabilized
Disability □ NML **E**xposure □ Exposed completely	**Blood glucose:** ________ □Glucose □Naloxone **Responsiveness:** □ A □ V □ P □ U **GCS:** ____ (E____ V____ M____) □Qualified **Moves Extremities:** □ LUE □RUE □LLE □RLE **Pupil:** Size: L________ R________ Reactivity: L________ R________	**F**AST □ Not Indicated □ Not Available □ NML **Peritoneum:** □ Negative □ Indeterminate □ Free Fluid: ________ **Chest:** □ Negative □ Indeterminate □ Pneumothorax (R/L): ________ □ Pleural fluid (R/L): ________ □ Pericardial effusion

MEDICAL HISTORY: MVA History obtained from: Patient

Medications: □ Anticoagulant:________ □ Unknown
Other: None

Allergies: None □ Unknown

Last Menstrual Cycle: ________ G___P___ □ Unknown

Past Medical: □ HTN □ DM □ COPD □ Psych □ Renal Disease □ Unknown
Other: Unremarkable

Pregnant? (circle) Yes / No □ Reported □ Testing done
Last Tetanus: ________ □ Unknown
Substance Use: □Tobacco □Alcohol □ Drugs □ IV Drugs □ Unknown

Past Surgeries (type & date): None □ Unknown
Safe at home? ________

HISTORY OF PRESENT ILLNESS: Date of Injury: 11/10/Y-2 **Time:** 9 : 45 (24h format)

Place of injury: Intersection of Rt. 38 and Larchmont □ Unknown

Activity at time of injury: Driving □ Unknown

Mechanism of injury (select one or multiple):
□Road traffic incident: □ Driver □ Passenger □ Pedestrian
□ Airbag □ Seat belt □ Other vehicle restraint □ Helmet
□ Extricated Patient vehicle: ________
□ Ejected Hit by/crashed with: ________
□Fall from: ________ □Hit by falling object: ________
□Stab/Cut □Gunshot □Sexual Assault
□Other blunt force trauma (struck/hit): ________
□Suffocation, choking, hanging
□Drowning: ________ Life vest: Y / N
□Burn caused by: ________
□Poisoning/Toxic Exposure: ________
□Unknown □Other: ________

First care sought:
Prehospital care
□ None □ Layperson first aid □ Health care professional (EMT, medic)
Care given:

Other Details of Incident
□ Loss of consciousness (circle): <5 min 5-29 min 30-24 hr >24 hr
□ Head trauma: Y / N □ Neck trauma: Y / N
Other:

Intent: □ Unintentional or accidental □ Intentional: □Self harm □Assault
□ Legal process, political unrest or war □ Unknown
Assaulted by (see Reference Card): ________

Hours since last meal: ________ hours □ Unknown

Substance use within 6 hours of injury:
□ Unknown □ None □ Reported □ Evidence (positive test or clinical findings)
□ Alcohol □ Other Substance (if known): ________

PHYSICAL EXAM: (See Reference Card for normal findings. Do NOT mark NML unless all key elements are normal.)

☐NML	**General**		Detail area of injury:
☐NML	**Neuro/Psych**		
☐NML	**HEENT**		
☐NML	**Neck**	Patient reports sensitivity	
☐NML	**Respiratory**		
☐NML	**Cardiac**		
☐NML	**Abdominal**		
☐NML	**Pelvis**		
☐NML	**GU/Rectal**		
☐NML	**MSK**		
☐NML	**Skin**		

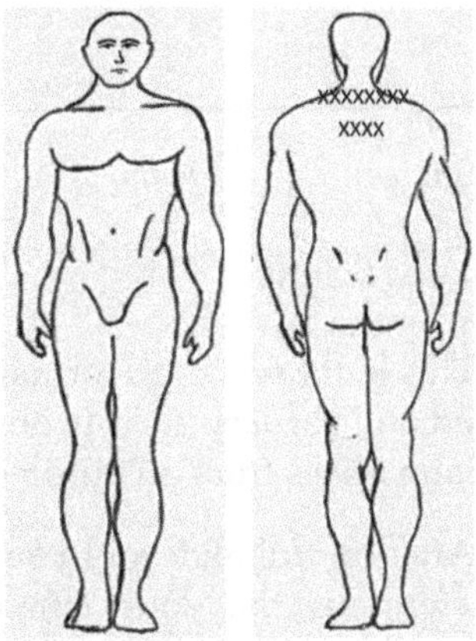

Form to be used with WHO Reference Card. See who.int/emergencycare for more information.

DIAGNOSTIC TESTS: Not indicated

UPT: ☐ Positive ☐ Negative ☐ N/A

Hgb: ____________ ☐ Result pending

Blood type: ____________

Other:

List imaging studies with results (and check findings below):

☐ Pneumothorax ☐ Pleural Fluid
☐ Pulmonary Opacity ☐ Rib Fracture
☐ Pelvic Fracture ☐ C-spine fracture
☐ Extremity Fracture

ADDITIONAL INTERVENTIONS: Not indicated

Fluids and Medications Given — **Time** (24h)

☐ IVF: ______ mLs ☐NS ☐LR ☐Other ________ ___:___
☐ Blood products (specify number of units given): ___:___
☐ Opioid Analgesia: ________ ___:___
☐ Other Analgesia: ________ ___:___
☐ Sedation/Paralytics: ________ ___:___
☐ Antibiotics: ________ ___:___
☐ Tetanus: ________ ___:___
☐ Other:

Procedures (circle and note outcome) — **Time** (24h):

☐ Intubation: ________ ___:___
☐ Chest Tube: ________ ___:___
☐ Splinting / Reduction: ________ ___:___
☐ Pelvic Stabilization: ________ ___:___
☐ Simple / Complex Laceration Repair: ________ ___:___
☐ Other:

ASSESSMENT (include summary and differential) **AND PLAN** (imaging; meds/interventions; consults with time called/arrived and recs):

Patient diagnosed with cervical sprain/strain (whiplash)
Patient advised to take over the counter NSAIDs and to follow up with primary care provider
Return to ED if symptoms worsen or change

REASSESSMENT at ___ ___:___ ___(24h) ☐ **Condition same**
Temp:_____ Pulse:_____ BP:___/___ RR:_____ SpO$_2$:____% on______ Changes:____________

DISPOSITION: Checklist completed: ☐ Y ☐ N ED departure (date & time): ___ 11 : 58 ___ (24h)

Diagnoses/Impressions (list all):

Number of serious injuries as judged by provider (circle): 0 1 ≥2

☐ **Admit to:** ☐ Ward ________ ☐ ICU ☐ OT
☐ **Discharge:** Plan discussed with patient? ☐ Yes ☐ No
☐ **Transfer to:** ____________
☐ **Left without being seen or before treatment complete**
☐ **Died of** (specify cause - NOT cardiopulmonary arrest): ____________

VS at Dispo at: 11 : 59 ___ (24h)
Temp: 98.9 Pulse: 73 BP: 97 / 70 RR: 14 SpO$_2$: 99 % on room

Accepting Provider: ____________

Emergency Unit Provider Name/Title (include handovers)	**Signature and Date**
Reed Fuller	*Reed Fuller* 11/10/Y-2

Skylar Schott
55 Main Street, Wildcat City

August 15, Y-0

Subject: *Denial of Administrative Claim*

Dear Skylar Schott:

This letter serves to formally deny your administrative claim for damages tendered on February 26, Y-0, on Standard Form 95. As noted on the claim form, your claim arises from an automobile collision that occurred on November 10, Y-2.

After careful review of your claim and supporting documentation, we have determined that your claim does not meet the requirements necessary to be compensable under the Federal Tort Claims Act. Specifically, our investigation did not reveal negligence on the part of the United States Postal Service driver involved in the collision. I have included the following documents which are part of this investigation: a text message from myself to the supervisor of the Wildcat City United States Postal Service Station, sent on August 10, Y-0; the USPS form of investigative report; and a photograph of the involved USPS vehicle taken on the day of the accident. Based on this information, as well as the information you provided, we did not conclude that the USPS driver was at fault for the accident. The USPS therefore denies the claim.

If you disagree with this decision, you have the right to file a lawsuit in the appropriate United States District Court within six months of the date of this letter.

Sincerely,
Kat McKee
USPS Agency Counsel
USPS National Tort Center
1720 Market Street, Room 2400
St. Louis, MO 63155-9948

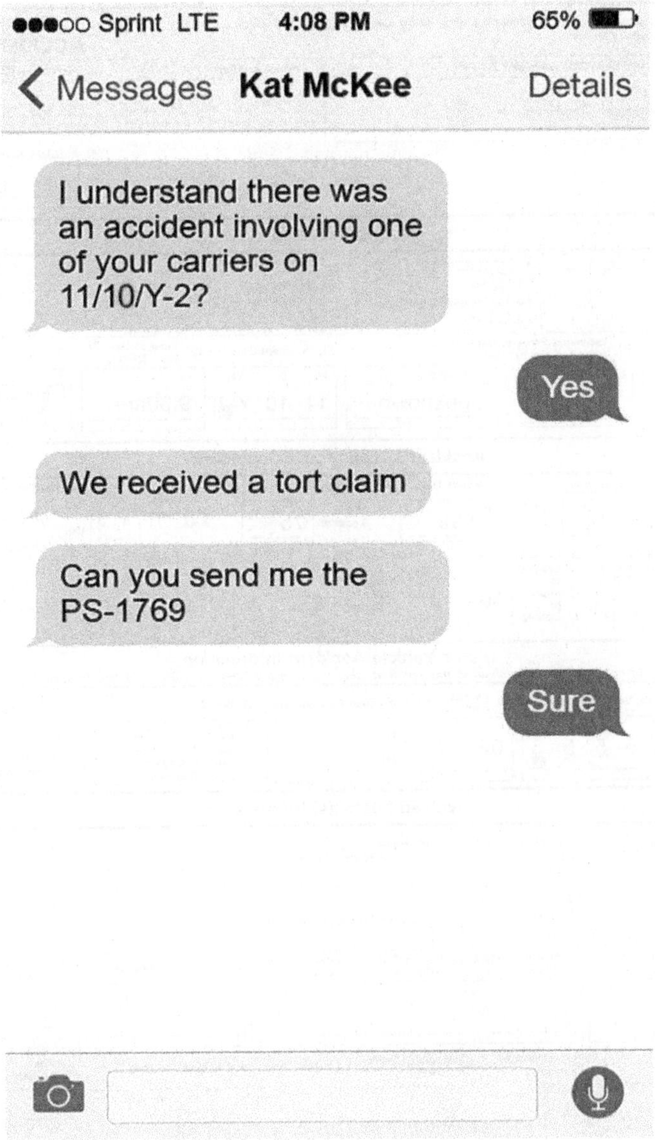
Sprint LTE
4:08 PM
65%
Messages
Kat McKee
Details
I understand there was an accident involving one of your carriers on 11/10/Y-2?
Yes
We received a tort claim
Can you send me the PS-1769
Sure

Carefully read instructions in the attached booklet. Items marked with an asterisk (*) must be answered using codes in the attached booklet.

U.S. POSTAL SERVICE
ACCIDENT REPORT

1. Post Office, Station, Branch, Unit (City, State and Zip+4): Wildcat City Postal Station
2. Finance Number: 5 5 5 5 5 5
3. Installation ID: 5 5 5 5
4. Accident Number: 0 0 1 1

General Information

5. Kind of Accident: 1. ☑ Motor Vehicle 2. ☐ Natural Event 3. ☐ Industrial 4. ☐ Other
6. Fire Involved? 1. ☑ No 2. ☐ Building & Contents 3. ☐ Other
7. Accident Resulted in: 1. ☐ Personal Injury Only 2. ☐ Property Damage Only 3. ☐ Personal Injury & Property Damage 4. ☑ No Case (No Injury/No Damage)
8. Was On-Site Investigation conducted by Immediate Supervisor? 1. ☑ Yes 2. ☐ No
9. Ownership of Damaged Property: a. Postal: 1 b. Non-Postal: 3
10. Estimated Property Damage (round to nearest dollar): a. Postal: $ 0 b. Non-Postal: $ unknown
11. Accident Date: Mo. 11 Day 10 Yr. Y-2
12. Time of Day–24 Hour Military: 9:30am
13. Day of Week: 1. ☐ Sun 2. ☐ Mon 3. ☐ Tues 4. ☐ Wed 5. ☑ Thurs 6. ☐ Fri 7. ☐ Sat

Accident Location and Conditions

14. Weather: 1
15. General Description of Accident Area: 3
Where Did Accident Happen?
16. Building: 99
17. Work Location: 75
18. Specific Description of Accident Area: 1
19. Rte/Sched/Op. No.: 19a Delivery Route 19b Emp. Op. No.
20. Light: 5
21. Surface: 2
22. Surface Conditions: 1
23. Circumstances Leading to Injury or Damage: 500
24. Item Causing Actual Injury or Damage: 032
25. Hazardous Situation Directly Related to Accident: 98
26. Defective or Hazardous Equipment or Material Related to the Accident: 98

Motor Vehicle Accident Information

(If no vehicle was involved in the accident, skip this section) (Items 28, 35 + 36 are reserved)

27. Total No. of Vehicles Involved: 2
28. (Reserved)
29. Vehicle Type: 5 5 5 5
30. Vehicle Path: 02
31. Were Seat Belts in Use? 1. ☑ Yes 2. ☐ No
32. Roll Over: 1. ☐ Without Collision 2. ☐ Before Collision 3. ☐ After Collision 4. ☑ No Roll Over
33. Employee Ejected from Vehicle: 1. ☐ Partial 2. ☐ Complete 3. ☑ Not Ejected
34. Area of Impact: 06

Involved Person(s) Information

37. Total No. of Accident Reports: 1
38. Person I.D. No.: 1
39. If Vehicle Accident Person Described Here Was: 1. ☐ Pedestrian 2. ☑ Driver 3. ☐ Passenger
40. Name (Last Name, First, MI): Unknown, left scene
41. Age:
42. Sex: 1. ☐ Male 2. ☐ Female
43. Des. & Activ.:
44. Injury/Illness Severity:
45. Nature of Most Severe Injury:
46. Part of Body Affected:
47. Unsafe Personal Factors:
48. Unsafe Practice:
49. Social Security No. (Employee Only):
50. Was Employee on Overtime Status? 1. ☐ Yes 2. ☑ No
51. Postal Service Experience: Years 2 Mos. 3
52. Hours of Safety Training: 65
53. Five Year Postal Accident Record: No. Prior Vehicle Accidents: 0 No. Prior Industrial Accidents: 0
54. Pay Location: 555
55. LDC/FON Code: 5555

Accident Factor(s) & Corrective Actions on Pages 1 & 2 of Form Have Been Reviewed & Are Concurred With.

56. Supervisor's Signature: Taylor Sutton Date: 11/10/Y-2 Supervisor's SSN: 555 - 55 - 5555
57. Next Higher Level Mgr. Signature: Date:
58. Supervisor's Printed Name: Taylor Sutton Telephone No.: (555)999-8765
59. MSC Safety Officer's Signature: Date:

PS Form **1769**, September 1991 (p. 1 of 2)

60. Is a JSA on File? 1. ☐ Yes 2. ☑ No **61. Preventive Action** 99 Accident Number 0 0 1 1 __ __

(Explain how the preventive action will eliminate or reduce cause(s) and prevent similar accidents)

N/A

Narrative/Complete Description of Accident

(Describe accident, events leading to accident, causes of injury or damage, and specific location of accident—Provide the ***who, what, when, where, why,*** *and* ***how*** *of this accident)*

Carrier was driving on Route 38 with a planned turn onto Larchmont Blvd.
Carrier indicated turn by signaling.
Intersection was clear and carrier began turn
Private vehicle was speeding, tried to beat carrier to the intersection
Carrier was already turning, private vehicle hit the back of the postal truck
Carrier checked for injuries and damages, called police and manager from scene
Police and other driver left scene before USPS management arrival

Hospital/Physician Information

Hospital/Physician Name	Address	Area Code & Telephone No.
N/A		
Treatment Date	Diagnosis	Duty Status

Hazardous Conditions and/or Equipment, Materials, Etc.

(Specify equipment with manufacturer name, model no., serial no., and year made. Where applicable, include vehicle ID no.)

None

Vehicle Diagram *(For use in motor vehicle accidents)*

(Indicate on the diagram below what happened. NOTE: Vehicle driven by postal employee is identified as Federal No. 1 regardless of ownership)

1. Number Federal vehicle as 1—other vehicle as 2—additional vehicle as 3, and show direction of travel by arrow *(Example:* → [1] [2] ← *)*
2. Use solid line to show path before accident —— [2]
   Broken line after accident - - - - - [2]
3. Show pedestrian by ——→ ○
4. Show railroad by ┼┼┼┼┼┼┼┼┼┼┼┼┼┼┼┼
5. Give names or numbers of streets or highways
6. Indicate north by arrow in this circle ——→ ○
7. Show point of impact by ——→ ×
8. Indicate skid marks & lengths
9. Indicate type & path of ejection
10. Traffic controls *(signals, sign, officer, etc.)*
11. Show width of roadway, traffic flow, parked vehicles, etc.

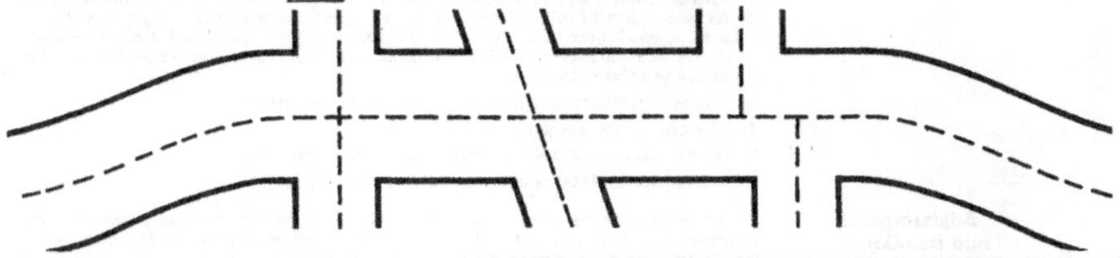

PS Form 1769, September 1991 *(p. 2 of 2)*

1-DETACH, FOLD AND SEND TO SERVICING SAFETY OFFICE

Form 1769

Accident Report

UNITED STATES POSTAL SERVICE

Instructions

General Information

The supervisor of the employee or operation involved must complete this form for all accidents regardless of extent of injury or amount of damage. Review all instructions and codes before completing this form. The Safety and Health office is available for assistance.

Information forwarded to the Office of Workers' Compensation Programs (OWCP) must not differ from information on this form.

Multiple Person Accidents

When more than one person is injured as a result of the accident, complete a separate form for each individual and use the same accident number on each form. Complete all items for the first person including the narrative. For additional persons involved, complete only Items 1-4, 37-55. Note: If more than one postal employee is involved in the accident, follow the instructions outlined above, regardless of whether there was injury or not.

Submission Procedures

1. **The supervisor must complete this form within 24 hours** of the date of the accident, the diagnosis of illness, or the date they were notified of the situation. The next level supervisor must verify all information on the form.
2. **The Manager, Safety and Health Services at the Division has the responsibility for reviewing the accuracy of the coding submitted on each PS Form 1769, *Accident Report,* or electronically entered into the Human Resources Information System (HRIS) Safety and Health Subsystem and accident log. If the codes on PS Form 1769 do not match with the narrative submitted by the supervisor of the employee or operation involved, the Manager, Safety and Health Services, is responsible for resolving the inconsistency.**
3. The installation head forwards the original accident report to the safety office within **3 calendar** days of the accident.
4. The local office must retain a copy of all reports (reportable or nonreportable) in that office for a 5-year period. Incorrectly filed or improperly coded 1769s may be returned to the originating office by the safety office. These must be corrected and resubmitted within 3 calendar days of receipt.
5. The safety office must:
   - review the completed form to ensure accuracy of codes;
   - coordinate any changes with the reporting office;
   - complete necessary items;
   - assign number and enter the accident information into the HRIS Safety and Health Subsystem within 1 calendar day of receipt, and;
   - retain the original copy for a period of 5 years.

Determining Reportable Accidents

The safety office assigns a number on all forms (Item 4), using HRIS guidelines, for both reportable and nonreportable incidents, including unadjudicated occupational illness cases, when it covers any of the following kinds of injuries, illnesses or damages:

1. All occupational traumatic injuries to postal employees regardless of whether the employee elects to file a Form CA-1 *(Federal Employee Notice of Traumatic Injury & Claim for Continuation of Pay/Compensation)* or a Form CA-6 *(U.S. Dept. of Labor — Official Superiors Report of Employee's Death)* is submitted to OWCP, and regardless of whether or **not** the OWCP claim is controverted.

   EXCEPTION: A First Aid case must be logged and coded "6" in Item 44 of this form. The report must be held as a nonreportable case at the safety office, when first aid care (NOT exceeding 2 visits) is provided by postal medical/health units or contract treating facilities unless the accident involves property damage such as may occur with a motor vehicle accident.

   NOTE: Cases with medical dispositions for limited duty are not to be coded as first aid injuries.
2. All occupational illnesses, including heart attacks, if a CA-2 *(Federal Employee's Notice of Occupational Disease and Claim for Compensation)* or CA-6 is submitted to OWCP.

   EXCEPTION: If an occupational illness, the form must be forwarded to the safety office for recording in the HRIS. These cases will be logged, assigned a reporting code and number, pending adjudication by the OWCP. Safety offices are to monitor OWCP decisions and amend the status of the case in the HRIS. Instructions for amendments/deletions are included in HRIS Safety and Health Updates.
3. Injuries or fatalities to non-postal persons on postal premises.
4. All motor vehicle accidents.
5. Property damage of $500 or more, regardless of ownership.
6. Fire damage of $100 or more regardless of ownership.

Adjustments and Deletions

Whenever there is a change in status, or if you discover an error in a previously filed 1769, within 3 calendar days send a copy of the Form 1769 and written justification and documents supporting the amendment/deletion to the servicing safety office for action.

PS Form **1769**, September 1991 *(p. 1 of 13 – instructions)*

Form 1769 (continued)

Instructions for Items 1-61

Item 1: **Post Office, Station, Branch, Unit** *(City, State & ZIP Code)* – Self-explanatory.

Item 2: **Finance Number** – Self-explanatory.

Item 3: **Installation ID** – The Installation ID is a 4-digit code.

Item 4: **Accident Number** – The safety office assigns numbers in ascending order, through HRIS, starting each FY with 0001, then 0002, etc. Keep a record of used numbers as duplicate or missing numbers will initiate unnecessary correspondence. Start with 0001 the following FY.

Item 5: **Kind of Accident** – Check the appropriate box.

Motor Vehicle – Any mechanically or electrically powered device designed for movement, not operated on rails, upon which or by which any person or property can be transported or drawn upon a land highway. The load on a motor vehicle is considered part of the vehicle.

Do **not** consider equipment such as vehicles operated on fixed rails, fork lifts, bicycles, or similar equipment as motor vehicles.

A motor vehicle accident is any accident involving a motor vehicle which is operated on official postal business, regardless of the ownership of the vehicle and which results in death, injury or property damage of one dollar or more, unless the vehicle is legally parked *(see note below)*. Who was injured, what property was damaged or to what extent, where the accident occurred, or who was responsible is not a factor.

NOTE: A legally parked vehicle is one in which the engine is turned off, the driver is not operating the controls, and the vehicle is parked where it is legal to do so. Temporarily "stopping" a vehicle without turning off the ignition, to load or unload mail, property, or persons, or a vehicle stopped at a sign, signal, police signal, or stalled in traffic, does not constitute a legally parked vehicle. If special written permission has been granted by law enforcement or municipal authorities to park in designated "No Parking" areas, and the postal vehicle is otherwise properly parked, the event may be classified as a parked industrial accident.

Natural Event – A natural event accident is any occurrence limited solely to property damage caused by such natural events as hurricane, flood, lightning, earthquake, volcano, hail, etc.

Other – This code is used to identify incidents involving vandalism or where only a non-employee was in an accident on postal premises. It shall not be used for incidents involving "on duty" postal employees. Example: A customer falls in a postal lobby.

Item 6: **Fire Involved** – Check appropriate box on the form: if box 2 or 3 is checked, Item 23 must be a fire code (#300-369).

1. – None.

2. – Building and Contents refers to any type of structure as well as all equipment, vehicles, stores, supplies, or material on, under, or within the structure.

3. – Other includes open storage, fires in collection or relay boxes, vehicles, or any other fires not in a building.

Item 7: **Accident Resulted in** – Check applicable box. If box 2 or 3 is checked also complete items 9 & 10. If box 4 is checked, this is a no incident, nonreportable case. There is no requirement to file a report. That is, no injury or property damage occurred as a result of incident.

Item 8: **Was On-Site Investigation Conducted By Immediate Supervisor?** – Check one.

PS Form **1769**, September 1991 *(p. 2 of 13 – instructions)*

Form 1769 (continued)

Item 9: **Ownership of Damaged Property** – If there was property damage select appropriate codes from the lists below:

a. **Postal**

0 – Not Applicable
1 – Postal

b. **Non-Postal**

0 – Not Applicable
2 – Other government agency
3 – Private party
4 – Employee's personal property used in postal operation, including privately owned rural carrier vehicles
5 – Hired, leased, or rented
6 – Contractor working on premises
7 – Star route or messenger
8 – Other *(explain in narrative)*
9 – Combination of the above

Item 10: **Estimated Property Damage (round to nearest dollar)** – *(For example, $987.65 must be written as* $ 0 0 0 9 8 8*)* –When possible, coordinate estimates with the managers of fleet operations, plant maintenance or procurement services.

a. Enter all postal damage here.
b. Enter all non-postal damage here. *(including privately owned rural carrier vehicles)*

Item 11: **Accident Date** – Use numerals. For example, February 28, 1991, must be written as 02/28/91.

Item 12: **Time of Day Accident Happened** – Use 24 hour clock. For example, 1:05 PM must be written as 1305, or 1:45 PM must be written as 1345.

Item 13: **Day of Week** – Check one.

Item 14: **Weather** – Enter the code from the following list that best describes the weather at the accident scene.

1. – Clear
2. – Cloudy
3. – Rain
4. – Snow
5. – Fog
6. – Sleet
9. – Not applicable *(if accident happened indoors)*

Item 15: **General Description of Accident Area** – Enter the code from the following list that best describes the neighborhood.

1. City business
2. City residential
3. Suburban business
4. Suburban residential
5. Rural
9. Not Applicable (use this code when accident occurs on postal premises)

Item 16: **Building Where Accident Happened** – If the accident happened in, or on the premises of a specific building, enter the appropriate code from the following list:

Postal

Associate Office

01 Category A-G P.O.
03 Category H-J P.O.
05 Category K P.O.
06 Category L P.O.

Station/Branch

02 Category A-G
04 Category H-J

07 Division - Main Office
08 MSC - Main Office
10 Vehicle Maintenance Facility
11 Airmail Facility
12 Regional Office
13 Headquarters Office
14 Postal Data Center
15 Supply Center
16 Mail Equipment Shop
18 Independent Mail Processing Center
19 Mail Bag Depository and Repair Center
22 Railroad Terminal
23 Truck Terminal
24 Bulk Mail Center
25 Postal Training Facility
26 Other

Non-Postal

50 Other government building
51 Customer's building/premises
97 Other *(Explain in narrative)*
99 Not applicable

PS Form 1769, September 1991 *(p. 3 of 13 - instructions)*

Form 1769 (continued)

Item 17: **Work Location** – Enter the code from the following list that best describes the type of work area or type of route where the employee was working.

On Postal Premises

01	Facing tables	**33**	Cancellation
02	Processing metered mail	**34**	Dispatching; staging area
03	Outgoing letter primary	**35**	Outgoing newspaper
04	Outgoing letter secondary	**36**	Incoming newspaper
06	Outgoing flat primary	**37**	Sack examination area
07	Outgoing flat secondary	**38**	NMO and irregulars
09	Outgoing parcel post primary	**39**	OCR – optical character reader
10	Outgoing parcel post secondary	**40**	Bar Code Sorter
12	Outgoing small parcels & rolls primary	**42**	Office work
13	Outgoing small parcels & rolls secondary	**43**	Miscellaneous non-mail handling activities by Mailing Division employees
15	Incoming letter primary	**45**	Computerized Forwarding System
16	Incoming letter secondary	**47**	Registry
17	Incoming flat primary	**48**	Carrier—office work
18	Incoming flat secondary	**49**	Dock & platform area
19	Incoming parcel post primary	**51**	Sorting machine cat walks, drive platform, and maintenance areas
20	Incoming parcel post secondary	**52**	Flat sorting machine (FSM)
21	Sack shakeout; dumping	**55**	Others relating to fixed-mechanization
22	Rewrap	**56**	Office area
23	Box section/letter casing	**57**	Small parcel and bundle sorter
24	Letter sorting machine (LSM)	**58**	Walk-in vault
25	Parcel sorting machine	**59**	Banding unit
26	Container loaders/unloaders	**60**	Lobby or customer areas
27	Weighers section and related activities	**61**	ET, MPE shops
28	Roller tables	**62**	Carpenter shops
29	Sack sorting machine	**63**	Battery shop
30	Rotary slides	**64**	Industrial vehicle shop
31	Chutes	**65**	Custodial equipment room
32	Culling operation	**66**	Other Maintenance area *(Explain in narrative)*
		67	Parking/Maneuvering area
		68	Aisle/Passageway

Off Postal Premises

69	Express Mail route	**78**	Air route
70	Foot route	**79**	Relay route
71	Special delivery route	**80**	Park and loop
72	Parcel post delivery	**81**	Depot
73	Mounted route delivery	**82**	Maintenance
74	Collection route	**83**	Enroute to servicing
75	Rural route	**84**	Enroute from servicing
76	Interstation route	**85**	Parking—maneuvering area
77	Intercity route		

Miscellaneous

87	Lunchroom/cafeteria	**92**	Elevator
88	Rest room	**93**	Mail box
89	Boiler room	**94**	Conveyor tunnel
90	Machine room	**97**	Other
91	Trash room or area	**99**	Not applicable

Item 18: **Specific Description of Accident Area** – Enter the code from the following list that best describes the description of the accident area:

1	Public street/road	**6**	Private road
2	Public sidewalk	**7**	Highway
3	Public alley	**8**	Expressway
4	Non-Postal premises	**9**	Postal premises
5	(Reserved)		

Item 19: **Route/Schedule/Operation Number** – Enter the route/schedule/operation number on which the employee was working at the time of the accident. If the employee was not on a route or schedule, enter the operation number.

Item 20: **Light** – Enter the code from the following list that best describes the type of light in which the accident occurred.

01	Dawn	**04**	Light provided but out
02	Dark and unlighted	**05**	Daylight—clear
03	Lighted or illuminated	**06**	Daylight—overcast
		07	Dusk

PS Form **1769**, September 1991 *(p. 4 of 13 – instructions)*

Form 1769 (continued)

Item 21: **Surface** — Enter the code from the following list that best describes the type of surface on which the accident occurred.

01	Concrete	07	Wood
02	Blacktop	08	Metal
03	Brick and stone	09	Sand
04	Gravel	10	Grass
05	Dirt	11	Other *(Explain in narrative)*
06	Tile	12	Carpet

Item 22: **Surface Conditions** — Enter the code from the following list that best describes the surface conditions on which the accident occurred.

01	Dry	06	Oily or slick
02	Wet	08	Icy
03	Muddy	09	Uneven or potholes
04	Snow	10	Other *(Explain in narrative)*
05	Loose sand or dirt		

Item 23: **Circumstances Leading to Injury or Damage** — Enter the code from the following list that best describes the action or condition which caused the accident.

Industrial

General
001 Caught in, under or between
002 Stepping in or on object *(not falling)*
003 Tripping on or tripped by object *(not falling)*
004 Slipping and twisting *(not falling)*
005 Exposure to extreme temperatures
006 Inhalation
007 Striking against material or equipment
008 Jumping to or from places
009 Stooping/bending

Animals
010 Dog bite
011 Dog incident *(other than bite)*
012 Other animal bite
013 Other animal incident *(not bites)*
014 Insect bite/sting

Contact with
020 Toxic substances
021 Caustic substances
022 Radiological substances
023 Biological substances *(no syringe)*
024 Biological substances *(syringe)*
025 Electric current
026 Chemical *(including dog spray)*
027 Hot or cold objects or substances
028 Dust/foreign particle

Falls on same level
040 To floors
041 To sidewalks/ground
042 To street

Falls from elevation
050 On stairs/steps
051 From platforms
052 From porches
053 From docks
054 From curbs
055 From ramps
056 From chairs, stools
057 From stationary vehicles
059 Into floor openings

Lifting, pulling, pushing, throwing, keying
080 Lifting from or to a higher level
081 Handling at same level
090 Pulling from or to a higher level
091 Pulling at same level
100 Pushing from or to a higher level
101 Pushing at same level
110 Throwing from or to a higher level
111 Throwing at same level
120 Repetitive motions/keying
121 Repetitive motions-other

Struck by
150 Falling objects
151 Flying objects
152 Material or equipment

Violence/Vandalism
160 By postal employee(s)
161 By others

Legally Parked/Other
170 On roadway
171 Off roadway
172 Rural carrier—off duty vehicle-related

Fires or Smoldering

Electricity
300 Short circuit in wiring
301 Overloaded wiring or switch
302 Defective wiring
303 Motors or equipment
309 Other *(Explain in narrative)*

Explosion
310 Carburetor backfire
311 Chemical
312 Bomb
319 Other *(Explain in narrative)*

Exposure
320 From adjoining premises or space

Flammable liquids
330 Flooded carburetor
339 Other *(Explain in narrative)*

Other
350 Incendiarism *(deliberately set fire)*
351 Lightning with fire ensuing
352 Matches and smoking
353 Open flames, welding & torches
354 Overheated grease, tar, or wax *(Example: hot box)*
355 Spontaneous ignition
356 Stoves, furnaces and boilers
368 Miscellaneous known causes
369 Undetermined cause of fire or smoldering

PS Form **1769**, September 1991 *(p. 5 of 13 – instructions)*

Form 1769 (continued)

Item 23—Continued:

Motor Vehicle

400 Rollaway—engine off
401 Runaway—engine on

500 Collision or sideswipe with another vehicle—both vehicles in motion.

600 Collision or sideswipe with a standing vehicle or Stationary object

700 Non-collision accidents

800 Not Elsewhere Classified

Item 24: **Item Causing the Actual Injury or Damage** — Select the code from the following list that best describes the actual article which inflicted the physical injury or damage to property. *(Specify manufacturer name, model no., etc. in narrative)*

Vehicle Powered
001 Aircraft
005 Watercraft
009 Railroad

Specific Part of Highway Motor Vehicle
010 Windshield
011 Instrument panel—dashboard
012 Delivery tray
013 Driver's seat
014 Rider's seat
015 Steering wheel or column
016 Foot pedals
017 Doors
018 Windows
019 Top structures
020 Floor structures
021 Cargo gate
022 Partition
023 Mirrors
024 Gear shift
026 Visors
027 Door or window handles
028 Moving cargo
029 Cargo restraints
030 Operator restraints
031 Fenders
032 Bumpers
033 Wheels
034 Grill
035 Hood

Containers
040 General purpose mail container (GPMC)
041 BMC/OTR
042 BMC/In-house
043 Letter tray transport
044 Eastern Region mail container (ERMC)
045 Large hampers with wheels *(1046)*
046 Small hampers with wheels *(1033)*
047 Wire mesh container
049 Other container

Vehicles—Industrial Powered
050 Fork lift
051 Tug
052 Tractor
053 Verti lift
054 Personnel Carriers
055 Pallet lift

Vehicles—Industrial Not Powered
061 Dollies
062 Warehouse trucks *(2-wheeled hand trucks, some with folding nose)*
063 Caddy carrier cart
066 Nutting/platform truck
067 Utility cart
069 Other, industrial vehicles—not powered

Mechanical Power Transmission Devices
070 Gears
071 Belts
072 Chains, ropes, cables
073 Drums, pulleys, sheaves
079 Other mechanical power transmission devices

Hand Tools
080 Not powered
081 Drills
083 Grinder, buffer, sander
085 Saw
087 Hammers, riviter, air/pneumatic
089 Other hand tools

Machines Powered
100 Buffers, polishers, sanders, grinders
101 Cancelling machines
102 Tying *(Plastic Strapping)*
106 Tying *(string)*
130 Electric arc welder
132 Drill press
138 Sander
140 Saw, circular
142 Saw, band
201 Tray mail conveyors
203 Other tray mail mechanization
204 Belt conveyors, parcels, sacks, and pouches
208 Sack sorting machines
209 Parcel sorting machines - fixed
210 Small parcel and bundle sorting machine
211 Monorail conveyors
212 Towveyors
213 Diverters
216 Extendable conveyors
218 Chutes, slides or roller tables
220 Automatic fine culler
221 Other mail preparation mechanization
222 SPLSM
223 Other conveyors—powered
224 Other fixed mechanization
225 Portable conveyors
227 MPLSM—excluding dropper assembly
228 MPLSM—dropper assembly
229 OCR Model KC2B
230 OCR Model 3560-PB
231 OCR Model 885
232 OCR Other Models

PS Form 1769, September 1991 *(p. 6 of 13 - instructions)*

Form 1769 (continued)

Item 24—Continued:

Machines Powered, (Continued)
233 BCS Model RA-9
234 BCS Model 880
260 BCS Model DBCS-990
261 BCS Model 925
235 BCS Other Models
236 FSM Model 775
237 FSM Other Models
238 Facer Canceler Mark II
239 Facer Canceler M-36
270 Facer Canceler FAM-885
240 Facer Canceler—Other Letter Mail
241 Flats Canceler—Model 15
242 Flats Canceler—Other Models
243 Vending Machines/Changers
244 Hamper Dumper
245 Pallet Dumper
246 Shoring Machine
247 Heat Seal Machine
248 Scissor Lift
249 Driverless Tractor
250 Keyboards *(typewriters, word processors, MPLSM Consoles, etc.)*
251 Video Display Terminal
299 Other machines not listed above

Miscellaneous
400 Acids
403 Alcohol
406 Animals *(other than dogs)*, example: birds
409 Atmosphere *(cold or hot)*
412 Barrels and drums
418 Benches/work
421 Boilers/pressure vessels
424 Books
427 Bottles
433 Carbon dioxide/monoxide
439 Cases
440 Chairs, LSM
441 Chairs, other
442 Chemicals, detergents and chemical compounds
445 Cleaning compounds/soap
448 Clips *(paper)*
451 Clothing
457 Conveyors—non-powered
460 Counters
461 Curbs
466 Debris/trash/scrap/waste materials
469 Desks *(lobby)*
475 Docks/platforms
476 Dock plates or boards
478 Dogs
481 Doors
484 Drugs/illegal

477 Dust
487 Electric apparatus *(other than tools)*
488 Elevator
490 Fasteners
497 File cabinets
493 Fire
496 Firearms
495 Floors
498 Foreign object
499 Furniture
502 Furnace
505 Gasoline
506 Ground
508 Guerney *(hamper—no wheels)*
511 Heaters *(space)*
514 Hoisting apparatus
515 Hose
407 Insects
517 Knives
520 Ladders
551 Lawn mower
552 Lockbox
523 Lock/key LA/holder/rotary
532 Lockers *(clothing)*
535 Lumber/wood products
541 Mail *(too large for canceling machine)*
547 Mail boxes *(collection & storage)*
548 Mail boxes *(customer)*
553 Mail pouch racks *(to hang empties)*
556 Mail sack *(loose not bundled)*
557 Medicine
562 Newspapers *(bundled)*
564 Paper
565 Oil/petroleum products
568 Pallets/skids
566 Plastic bands/strapping
567 Porch
574 Rest bars
575 Ring knife
576 Sack buckle-hasp
578 Scissors
579 Sharp instrument
580 Shoes
583 Smoke
444 Snow blower
446 Solvents
586 Staples
589 Steam

571 Stoves
590 Steps/stairs
592 Tire(s)
593 Welding slag/spark
601 Windows
605 Trees/branches/limbs
606 Stools
607 Sidewalks/street
608 Rubber bands

Boxes, crates and containers
710 Less than 10 lbs
711 11-20 lbs
712 21-40 lbs
713 41-70 lbs
714 71 lbs and over

Mail Trays
740 Less than 10 lbs
741 11-20 lbs
742 21-40 lbs
743 41-70 lbs
744 71 lbs and over

Mail Sack/Pouch
760 Less than 10 lbs
761 11-20 lbs
762 21-40 lbs
763 41-70 lbs
764 71 lbs and over

Satchels
770 Less than 10 lbs
771 11-20 lbs
772 21-40 lbs
773 41-70 lbs
774 71 lbs and over

Other material/equipment
780 Less than 10 lbs
781 11-20 lbs
782 21-40 lbs
783 41-70 lbs
784 71 lbs and over

999 Other *(Explain in narrative)*

PS Form **1769**, September 1991 *(p. 7 of 13 – instructions)*

Form 1769 (continued)

Item 25: **Hazardous Situation Directly Related to Accident** — Enter the code from the following list that best describes hazardous situations directly related to the accident.

01	Inadequate aisle or working space
02	Congested or blocked area
03	Unmarked doors *(In-Out)*
04	Poor drainage
05	Unsafe *(for working condition)* dress or apparel
06	Insufficient electrical outlets
07	Inadequately guarded equipment
08	Absence of hand rails on steps or ramps
09	Poor housekeeping *(cluttered and disorderly)*
10	Unsafe planning lay-out or operational methods
11	Improper or insufficient lighting
12	Lack of emergency lighting
13	Dangerous arrangement of loading areas, collection box location, etc.
14	Excessive noise
15	Platforms too high or too low
16	Lack of personal protective equipment
17	Absence of steps to and from platform
18	Improper ventilation
19	Excessive wax on floors
20	Hazardous conditions of customer's premises
21	Slippery or uneven surface
22	Unrestrained animals
23	Overload equipment
24	Faulty construction
30	Incorrect equipment design
31	Faulty job training
32	Improper assignment of personnel
33	Lack of or unspecified job procedures
34	Lack of or unspecified safety rules
35	Lack of knowledge or skill
51	Sight obstruction
52	Improperly loaded equipment or vehicle
62	Absence of maintenance platforms
63	Absence of or insufficient drive chain *guards or gear guards*
65	Absence of or insufficient drive enclosure screening or access interlock switches
67	Absence of or insufficient emergency pull cords or stop buttons
69	Improperly located or inaccessible lubrication points
70	Improperly located or inaccessible emergency pull cords or stop buttons
72	Other hazardous situations relating to mechanized equipment
97	Other hazardous situation *(Explain in narrative)*
98	No hazardous situations

Item 26: **Defective or Hazardous Equipment or Material Related to Accident** — Enter the code from the following list that best describes hazardous equipment or material that was related to the accident.

Motor Vehicle

01	Defective accelerator
02	Defective clutch
03	Defective foot brakes
04	Defective hand brakes
05	Defective horn
06	Defective springs or suspension system
07	Defective or dirty windshield
08	Defective windshield wipers
09	Defective or poorly adjusted mirrors
10	Defective steering system
11	Defective exhaust system
12	Defective seat
13	Defective safety belts
15	Defective headlights
16	Defective directional signals
17	Defective stop *(brake)* lights
18	Defective wheels
20	Smooth or worn tires
21	Under/over inflated tires
22	Motor failure
23	Poor stability *(vehicle)*
24	Restricted vision *(part of vehicle design)*
26	Defective wiring
27	Defective shift selector

Industrial

40	Short circuit in wiring
41	Defective or overloaded wire or switch
44	Defective premises of customers
50	Sharp edges on equipment and furniture
51	Defective ring knife
52	Ragged or rusty mail boxes
53	Defective cord on sacks
54	Defective postal stairs/steps
55	Defective customer stairs/steps or porches
56	Structural failure
57	Rough, slippery or broken walking surfaces
58	Loose material on surface
60	Malfunction of door safety interlocks
61	Malfunction of emergency pull cords or stop buttons
63	Malfunction of other safety equipment
64	Defective latches—mail containers receptacles

Industrial Powered Vehicles

65	Defective shift selector
66	Defective brakes

Other

97	Other defects *(Explain in narrative)*
98	No defects or hazardous equipment or material

Item 27: **Total Number of Vehicles** — Enter the total number of vehicles involved in the accident.

Item 28: **Reserved.**

PS Form **1769**, September 1991 *(p. 8 of 13 – instructions)*

Form 1769 (continued)

Item 29: **Vehicle Type** – For postal-owned vehicles enter the make/model code number from the most recent Fleet Management Bulletin. Be sure to use all 4 digits.

If the accident involved **non-postal vehicles**, enter a code from the following list.

0091 Contract
0092 Leased
0093 Private–drive out agreements
0094 Private–rural carriers *(LHD)*
0095 GSA
0096 Private–rural carriers *(RHD)*
0098 Other vehicles used on official Postal operations
0099 All others–non postal

Item 30: **Vehicle Path** – Enter the code from the following list that best describes the movement of the vehicle immediately preceding the accident.

01 Straight ahead
02 Left turn
03 Right turn
04 U-turn right
05 U-turn left
06 Passing
07 Being passed
08 Backing
09 Slowing
10 Stopped
11 Skidding
12 Jackknifing
13 Running off road
14 Pulling to curb/mailbox
15 Pulling from curb/mailbox
16 Unattended vehicle moving
17 Unattended vehicle stopped
18 Legally parked
19 Entering curve
20 Changing lane
47 Other *(Explain in narrative)*
49 Not applicable

Items 31-33: **Self-explanatory.**

Item 34: **Initial Area of Impact**

Passenger Cars, Jeeps, LLVs, Trucks (Excluding 5 & 7-Ton Trucks & Tractor Trailers)

01 Front end
02 Right front side
03 Left front side
04 Right occupant side
05 Left occupant side
06 Right rear side
07 Left rear side
08 Rear end
09 Top structure
10 Under carriage

5-Ton or Larger Trucks and Tractor Trailers ONLY

11 Front end
12 Right front side
13 Left front side
14 Right occupant side
15 Left occupant side
16 Right front cargo side
17 Left front cargo side
18 Right rear cargo side
19 Left rear cargo side
20 Rear end
21 Top structure
22 Under carriage
97 Other, regardless of vehicle size *(Explain in narrative)*

Items 35 & 36: **Reserved.**

Item 37: **Total No. of Accident Reports** – One form must be submitted for each person injured. See "Multiple Person Accidents", p. 1 of Instructions.

Item 38: **Person Identification No.** – If only one person was injured in the accident enter "1". For each additional injured person, complete an additional 1769, numbering each consecutively in this space. See "Multiple Person Accidents", p. 1 of Instructions.

Item 39: **Self-explanatory.**

Item 40: **Name** – Name of person involved in accident.

Item 41: **Age** – If the actual age of a non-postal person is unknown, enter an estimated age.

Item 42: **Self-explanatory.**

Item 43: **Designation and Activity** – Enter the 3-digit DES/ACT code for the employee in the space provided. For non-postal, enter one of the codes below:

001 Customer or general public
002 Non-postal Government employee

Item 44: **Injury/Illness Severity** – Enter the code from the following list that best describes the type of injury, if any, experienced by the person identified in item 40 of this form.

Postal Employees

1. **Fatality:** A fatality is any work-related injury or illness which results in death, regardless of the time between the injury and death, or length of illness. If death occurs after submission of an Accident Report you must change the severity code in the HRIS.
2. **Lost-Workday Case:** A lost-workday case results from a work-related injury or illness severe enough to render an employee unable to perform any duties on any workday or workdays, consecutive or not, after the day of injury or diagnosis of illness during which the employee would have worked but could not because of the injury or illness.

Form 1769 (continued)

Item 44—Continued

3. **Lost-Time-Limited-Duty Case:** A lost-time-limited-duty case is any work-related injury or illness severe enough to cause an employee to be unable to work the number of daily or weekly hours that the employee would normally work on any day after the day of injury or diagnosis of illness. For example: a full-time employee who works less than 8 hours a day, or less than 40 hours a week; or part-time employee who normally averages 30 hours a week, but can only work 15 hours a week because of the injury or illness.

4. **No-Lost-Workday-Case:** A no-lost-workday-case is any work-related injury or illness which requires medical treatment and which does not result in a fatality, lost workday, limited duty, first aid, termination, or permanent reassignment case.

5. **A No-Lost-Time-Limited-Duty Case:** A no-lost-time-limited-duty case is any work-related injury or illness which results in a limited duty assignment and does not reduce the number of hours the employee would normally work. For example: an employee assigned to other duties in the same craft, another craft, or other installation without any reduction of hours *normally worked*, on any day after the date of injury or diagnosis of illness.

6. **A First Aid Case:** A first aid case is normally any work-related minor injury that requires no more than two medical visits, the second of which is to confirm full recovery. Form 1769 must be completed for all first aid injury cases, both reportable and nonreportable. All first aid cases must be logged and coded "6" in Item 44. First aid care not exceeding two visits provided by the **postal medical officer or contract physician** is recorded as *nonreportable* in the HRIS. First aid care provided by the employee's private physician or emergency room or other treating facilities, for which medical payment will be made through OWCP, must be logged and recorded as a *reportable* case in HRIS and coded "6" in Item 44.

   All motor vehicle accidents resulting in property damage or personal injury, including first aid, are reportable.

   Cases resulting in a medical disposition of disability and/or limited duty assignment, regardless of the number of medical visits, are *not* to be recorded as first aid cases. For reporting purposes, when employees sustain an injury but decline treatment, the case is to be logged and recorded in the HRIS as a nonreportable first aid case. Examples of first aid treatment are:

   A. Application of antiseptic on the first visit to a doctor or nurse. It does not matter whether the doctor or nurse is located at a postal medical unit, private physician's office, public or private clinic, or a hospital.
   B. Bandaging.
   C. Treatment for first-degree burns.
   D. Application of compress, hot or cold.
   E. Use of an elastic bandage.
   F. Irrigation of the eye to remove foreign bodies not embedded.
   G. Removal of foreign bodies from a wound by tweezers or other simple techniques.
   H. Administration of non-prescription medications.
   I. Observation of injury.
   J. Applications of ointments to abrasions to prevent drying or cracking.
   K. Tetanus shots, initial or boosters alone.
   L. X-ray, if negative.

NOTE: Do not consider any injury involving loss of consciousness, restriction of work or motion, or reassignment to another job as a first aid case.

7. Termination or permanent reassignment involving a lost workday case.

8. Termination or permanent reassignment involving a lost time-limited duty case.

9. Termination or permanent reassignment not involving a lost workday or lost time-limited duty case.

0. No injury

Non-Postal People

x. **Non-postal fatality**

y. **Non-postal injury**

z. No injury

PS Form **1769**, September 1991 *(p. 10 of 13 – instructions)*

Form 1769 (continued)

Item 45: **Nature of Most Severe Injury or Illness** — Select the code from the following list that best describes the nature of the injury or illness.

Injury Codes:

- **00** No injury
- **01** Amputation
- **02** Removal of eye
- **03** Asphyxia/suffocation
- **05** Drowning
- **06** Bites *(animals or insects)*
- **07** Burns *(hot substances)*
- **08** Burns *(chemicals, acids, etc.)*
- **09** Burns *(radiation, sunburn, etc.)*
- **10** Concussion *(or any head blow causing unconsciousness)*
- **11** Contusion *(bruise, crushing—skin intact)*
- **12** Cuts *(open wounds—greater than scratches)*
- **13** Abrasion/scratch(es)
- **14** Dislocation
- **15** Electric shock
- **16** Fractures or breaks
- **18** Gunshot wounds
- **20** Heart attack
- **21** Ruptured disc
- **22** Hernia-rupture
- **23** Strain
- **24** Sprain
- **39** Other injury *(Explain in narrative)*
- **40** Foreign objects in eye(s)

Occupational Illness Codes: An occupational illness of an employee is any abnormal condition or disorder caused by exposure to environmental factors associated with the employment over a period longer than a single workday or shift.

- **60** **Occupational Stress**
- **61** **Occupational Skin Diseases or Disorders.** Examples: Contact dermatitis, eczema, or rash caused by primary irritants, and sensitizers or poisonous plants; oil acne; chrome ulcers; chemical burns or inflammations; etc.
- **62** **Dust Diseases of the Lungs *(Pneumoconioses).*** Examples: Silicosis, asbestosis, coal worker's pneumoconisis, byssinosis, and other pneumoconioses.
- **63** **Respiratory Conditions Due to Toxic Agents.** Examples: Pneumonitis, pharyngitis, rhinitis or acute congestion due to chemicals, dusts, gases, or fumes; farmer's lung; etc.
- **64** **Poisoning. *(Systematic Effects of Toxic Materials).*** Examples: Poisoning by lead, mercury, cadmium, arsenic, or other metals, poisoning by carbon monoxide, hydrogen sulfide or other gases; poisoning by benzol, carbon tetrachloride, or other organic solvents; poisoning by insecticide sprays such as parathion, lead arsenate; poisoning by other chemicals such as formaldehyde, plastics and resins, etc.
- **65** **Disorders Due to Physical Agents. *(Other Than Toxic Materials).*** Example: Heatstroke, sunstroke, heat exhaustion and other effects of environmental heat; freezing, frostbite and effects of exposure to low temperatures; caisson disease; effects of ionizing radiation *(isotopes, X-rays, radium)*; effects of nonionizing radiation *(welding, flash, ultraviolet rays, microwaves, sunburn)*. etc.

Disorders Due to Repeated Trauma. Examples: Synovitis, bursitis, Raynaud's phenomena and other conditions due to repeated motion, vibration or pressure.

- **66** **Tenosynovitis**
- **67** **Tendonitis**
- **68** **Carpal Tunnel Syndrome**
- **69** **Hearing Loss**
- **70** **Epicondylitis**
- **71** **De Quervains**
- **72** **Hand-Arm Vibration Syndrome**
- **98** **Other Disorders Due to Repeated Trauma**
- **99** **All Other Occupational Illnesses.** Examples: Anthrax, brucellosis, infectious hepatitis, malignant and benign tumors, food poisoning, histoplasmosis, occidioidomycosis, etc.

Item 46: **Part of Body Affected** — Select the code from the following list that best describes the body part which was affected by the most severe injury.

- **00** **Not applicable**

Head and Neck

- **01** Ear(s)
- **02** Eye(s)
- **03** Face
- **04** Skull, scalp
- **05** Nose
- **06** Tooth/Teeth/Mouth
- **09** Multiple head injuries *(combination from 01-06)*
- **16** Neck

Upper Extremities—Arm

- **20** Upper arm
- **21** Elbow
- **22** Lower arm
- **23** Multiple arm injuries *(combination from 20-22)*
- **24** Wrist
- **25** Hand(s)
- **26** Finger(s)
- **29** Multiple injuries *(combination from 01-26)*

PS Form 1769, September 1991 *(p. 11 of 13 - instructions)*

Form 1769 (continued)

Item 46—Continued:

Trunk
31 Abdomen *(include internal organs)*
32 Back
33 Chest *(include ribs, breast bone, and internal organs)*
34 Hips *(include pelvic organs and buttocks)*
35 Shoulder
39 Multiple trunk *(combination from 31-35)*

Lower Extremities—Leg
40 Thigh
41 Knee
42 Lower leg *(above ankle)*
43 Ankle
44 Foot *(not ankle or toes)*
45 Toe(s)
49 Multiple lower extremities *(combination from 40-45)*

Other Body Parts
50 Multiple parts *(more than one major area above)*
60 Circulatory system *(heart, arteries, veins, etc.)*
70 Respiratory system *(lungs, etc.)*
80 Nervous system/psychological
99 Insufficient information to identify part

Item 47:

Unsafe Personal Factors — If any of the following situations contributed to the accident, enter the corresponding code. If more than one apply, enter the one most responsible for the accident.

01 Didn't see *(Explain in narrative)*
02 Didn't hear *(Explain in narrative)*
03 Failure to comply with rules
05 Operating without authority
06 Using alcoholic beverage
07 Inadequate help for heavy lifting
09 Wilful disregard of instructions
10 Using drugs *(LSD, heroin, etc.)*
11 Horseplay
12 Fatigue
39 Other unsafe personal factor *(Explain in narrative)*
48 No unsafe personal factor
49 Not applicable

Item 48:

Unsafe Practice — Enter the code that best describes the unsafe practice that was most responsible for the accident and/or injury.

Industrial
01 Removing safety devices
02 Adjusting or cleaning moving equipment
03 Haste
04 Removing jam or clearing equipment *(without shutting off power)*
05 Using defective equipment
06 Not using protective equipment
07 Overloading
08 Unsafe carrying, placing, loading
09 Throwing material *(instead of carrying or passing)*
10 Inattention or distraction *(not caused by verifying or fingering mail)*
11 Inattention or distraction caused by fingering mail
12 Taking shortcuts
13 Pulling instead of pushing rolling equipment
14 Failure to correct known hazard
15 Failure to follow lockout procedures

Motor Vehicle
20 Jumping from moving vehicle
21 Stopping vehicle with parking brake instead of foot brake
22 Driving too fast for conditions
23 Driving in wrong lane
24 Passing in unsafe area
25 Running changing traffic light
26 Following too closely
27 Operating without eye glasses when required
28 Exceeding speed limit

Failure To
30 Seat passenger
31 Use safety belts
32 Check or adjust mirrors
33 Give proper signal
34 Check clearance
35 Yield right-of-way
36 Close vehicle door
37 Observe traffic sign or signals
38 Set handbrake
39 Keep both hands on wheel

Industrial and Motor Vehicle

Improper
40 Placing of mail *(on seat, tray, etc.)*
41 Securing of load
42 Starting and stopping
43 Backing
44 Parking
45 Turns
46 Lane changes
47 Use of equipment or materials
48 Verifying or fingering mail *(while walking up or down stairs or curbs, driving, or when crossing street)*
49 Lifting
50 Use of rest bars
87 Other unsafe practices *(Explain in narrative)*
88 No unsafe practice

PS Form 1769, September 1991 *(p. 12 of 13 – instructions)*

Form 1769 (continued)

Item 49: **Social Security Number** – Enter the employee's social security number. For non-postal persons enter all 9's.

Item 50: **Was Employee on Overtime Status?** – Check one.

Item 51: **Postal Service** – Round off length of years in the Postal Service to the nearest whole month and enter this number. For example: enter 1 year 6 months and 10 days as 01/06.

Item 52: **Hours of Safety Training** – Enter hours of safety training employee received within the last five years as recorded on PS Form 2548 – or other available records.

Item 53: **Self-explanatory.**

Item 54: **Pay Location** – Enter the pay location of the employee at the time of the accident. If not applicable enter "000".

Item 55: **LDC/FON Code** – Enter the LDC Code of the employee **at the time of the accident.** If not applicable enter "00". *(If you do not know the LDC Code, consult your timekeeper.)*
NOTE: You must enter a LDC Code (or "00"). If you do not, this 1769 will be returned. At a future date, instructions will be provided concerning the replacement of the LDC Code with the 4-digit FON Code.

Items 56–59: **Self-explanatory.**

Item 60: **Is A JSA (PS Form 1783, *On-the-Job Safety Review/Analysis*) On File?** – Indicate whether an analysis is on file for the job task being performed at the time of accident or injury.

Item 61: **Preventive Action Code** – Enter the code from the following list that best describes the action you will take to most effectively eliminate or reduce the accident cause(s) and prevent similar accidents.

01 Provide training/instruction to ensure that employee understands established job procedures and will recognize similar hazards or unsafe practices in the future.
02 Establish proper job procedures for task to be performed.
04 Simplify established job procedures if complex or unclear.
05 Ensure that employee has skill or knowledge to perform task.
06 Motivate employee to properly perform task.
07 Initiate work order.
08 Provide adequate hazard warning signs or notices.
09 Initiate action to determine if employee meets physical requirements of the job.
10 Formal discipline proposed.
11 Ensure adequate supervision.
12 Initiate action to improve/correct/repair equipment or layout design.
13 Initiate action to improve/correct equipment maintenance procedures or housekeeping.
14 Ensure availability of and/or provide proper protective equipment, materials, or tools.
15 Other *(Explain in narrative).*
16 Notify animal control authorities.
99 Not applicable.

Instructions for Narrative

Complete the narrative first and provide the information listed below. This will make it easier to select the proper codes.

Be specific and provide as much detail as possible when completing the narrative. Describe the specific task(s) which the employee was performing immediately prior to the accident, noting whether the task(s) was being properly performed. Indicate whether or not the employee was aware of a hazard and if so, describe exactly what the employee was doing at that time. Describe the employee's reaction to avoid the hazard, if any. Specifically describe the interaction between the employee and the hazard which caused the injury or property damage, and describe the resulting injury or property damage.

Hospital/Physician Information

If the accident resulted in an injury to the person named on this report, record the attending physician's name (if known), hospital and/or treating medical facility, address and phone number. Additionally, provide the date the employee received medical treatment and resulting diagnosis and work status.

Hazardous Conditions, and/or Equipment, Materials, Etc.

If the contributing cause of the accident was due to hazardous conditions and/or equipment or material, include the manufacturer's name, make and model number (vehicle ID number, where appropriate) of the equipment/material involved in the accident.

Vehicle Diagram

If the report involves a motor vehicle accident, diagram the accident on page 2 using the space provided. That is, show the direction of postal vehicle travel, point of collision with other vehicle, etc., and use items 1 through 11 of this section, as appropriate, to illustrate what happened.

PS Form **1769**, September 1991 *(p. 13 of 13 – instructions)*

We Deliver For You.
www.usps.com
UNITED STATES
POSTAL SERVICE

PART III

EXERCISES

CHAPTER 1

INITIAL CLIENT INTERVIEW

The initial interview between a lawyer and a client is a necessary and critical first step in the litigation process. This meeting serves two primary goals. First, it provides the lawyer with a venue to gather crucial information from the client. Second, it provides the client with an opportunity to understand the litigation process.

The meeting typically begins with the lawyer providing an introduction designed to build rapport with the client. The lawyer's goal is to get to know the client and to establish a comfortable, professional relationship with them. The rapport building is a two-way street; the client also gets to know the lawyer during this process. Establishing the relationship is critical for the lawyer. It helps foster open and honest communication, which is essential for successful and ethical litigation.

The lawyer then gathers information about the client and the dispute giving rise to the litigation. The lawyer asks the client to explain why the client sought legal assistance. The lawyer questions the client, seeking a description of the events, challenges, or disputes the client is facing. The lawyer listens carefully and asks follow-up questions to ensure a complete understanding. During this process, the lawyer may request specific documents or evidence to better learn the details of the case.

During this discussion, the lawyer must identify potential legal issues. For example, the lawyer should be aware of the applicable statute of limitations and should inquire about timing to confirm whether a complaint would be timely if filed.

Once the lawyer has gathered information from the client, the lawyer should provide information to the client. Based on the details shared by the client, the lawyer may offer an initial opinion on the case, discussing possible legal strategies and outlining the chances of success.

Even if the lawyer is not prepared to discuss the merits of the case during this initial meeting, the lawyer should nonetheless inform the client about the logistics of litigation. The lawyer should explain the legal process, timelines, and potential outcomes to help manage the client's expectations.

The lawyer should also discuss the legal fees and costs with the client. The lawyer should specify how fees will be calculated, whether that is on an hourly, flat-fee, or contingency basis. The lawyer should also provide details about payment schedules, retainer fees, and any other financial arrangements.

When meeting with a client, it is critical for the lawyer to explain the boundaries of the attorney-client privilege and confidentiality. The lawyer must also explain the parameters of the attorney-client relationship, including the lawyer's duty to represent the client's interests within the boundaries of ethical advocacy.

After this discussion, the lawyer should clarify the client's understanding as well as any objectives or concerns. The client should articulate a specific goal and the lawyer should provide feedback as to whether that goal is achievable. If the client has concerns, the lawyer should allay them to the extent possible without misrepresenting the realities of litigation.

The final part of the interview is for the lawyer to outline the next steps in the litigation process. This might include homework for the client if the client failed to bring necessary documents to the interview. It could also include tasks the lawyer will complete, such as filing a complaint or an answer. Both the lawyer and client should leave the interview understanding their responsibilities going forward.

EXERCISE 1: Π AND Δ

Assume you are meeting for the first time with your client or client representative (either Schott or Royal). Your firm or organization[1] has agreed to represent either Schott or the United States in civil litigation, but beyond this basic agreement nothing has yet been put into place to formalize your relationship. Your client or client representative has never been involved in litigation before and may have questions about the process and the scope of your representation.

Consider what you need to learn during this meeting to be prepared to litigate this case. After this meeting, you will need to draft an engagement letter as well as a complaint and/or answer, so think about these tasks and make sure you gather the necessary information from your client.

a) Draft a written outline for the interview.
   - Plaintiff's counsel (Π), draft an outline for an interview of Schott.
   - Defense counsel (Δ), draft an outline for an interview of Royal.

b) Conduct the interview.
   - Plaintiff's counsel (Π), interview Schott.
   - Defense counsel (Δ), interview Royal.

1. The United States is typically represented in FTCA cases by the U.S. Attorney's Office, a government agency, rather than by a private law firm. For purposes of litigating this case, you can either assume that a conflict of interest has prompted the U.S. Attorney's Office to refer this case to outside counsel, and that you work for a law firm, or you can assume that you are an Assistant United States Attorney. Your professor may provide you with background materials to bring you up to speed on the FTCA.

CHAPTER 2

ENGAGEMENT LETTER

The engagement letter, or retainer agreement, is a crucial part of establishing the attorney-client relationship. The engagement letter outlines the responsibilities and expectations of both the client and the attorney. Doing so protects both parties, as the client is aware of the limited scope of the representation, and the attorney is clear as to the payment of services. It is important that an engagement letter be completed for any client matter, no matter the practice area.

Crafting the scope of an engagement letter needs to be thoughtful. From the attorney's perspective, the scope of the matter must be clearly delineated. In addition to specific services to be provided, consider areas of representation that are specifically excluded. For instance, in litigation, all matters pertaining to the case at the bar may fall under the scope of the engagement letter, but appeals related to the matter are excluded. In transactional matters, the drafting of agreements may fall under the scope of the engagement letter, but litigation arising from those agreements is excluded. Defining excluded areas of representation provides the client with clear expectations regarding professional services.

In addition, fees associated with services under an engagement letter need to be discussed. The structure of fees will vary depending on the practice area, firm, and, sometimes, client. There is much leeway in devising fee structures, such as hourly billing, flat-fee billing, contingency fee structures, and combinations thereof. As an attorney, it is important to consider the expected time to be invested in a client matter and determine how best to capture that work from a cost perspective. Generally, plaintiff's work is structured on a contingency fee basis while defense work follows an hourly billing structure. These structures best fit the nature of each practice.

Other sections within an engagement letter to be considered include the client's right to terminate, the attorney's right to withdraw, governing law provisions, dispute resolution provisions, and the duties of the client. Some engagement letters will amount to a one-page agreement while others will comprise a several-page, letter-style document. Depending on the jurisdiction in which you practice, requirements for engagement letters may vary. Further, requirements may vary depending on the type of matter at hand. For instance, in New York, there are variants that apply to domestic relations matters as opposed to other civil matters. Therefore, it is important to become familiar with your jurisdiction's requirements for engagement letters.

EXERCISE 2: Π AND Δ

You have now met with your client or client representative (either Schott or Royal). Before you begin actively litigating this case, you will need to form an attorney-client relationship. As you have never represented this client before, you will need a robust and comprehensive engagement letter that will protect both your law firm and your client as you move forward. Draft the engagement letter.

- Plaintiff's counsel (Π), draft an engagement letter directed to Schott.
- Defense counsel (Δ), draft an engagement letter directed to Royal.

CHAPTER 3

COMPLAINT (PLAINTIFF'S COUNSEL ONLY)

A civil complaint is a specific type of legal document known as a pleading. The filing of a complaint begins the formal litigation process in most civil actions. It is typically the first filing in any civil action, so it is the plaintiff's chance to make a first impression on the defendant and the court.

The primary purpose of a complaint is to notify the defendant of the plaintiff's case. It provides notice to the defendant of the plaintiff's legal theories, informs the defendant of the facts supporting those theories that are already known to the plaintiff, narrows the issues for litigation, and gives the court an opportunity to weed out non-meritorious claims early in litigation.

Drafting the complaint, of course, is not the initial step in the litigation process for plaintiff's counsel. On the contrary, plaintiff's counsel has a responsibility to conduct a reasonable investigation to ascertain the facts of the case and to ensure that the cause of action is not false or frivolous. Counsel will also need to research the law. Failing to do an appropriate investigation prior to filing a complaint can result in a false or frivolous filing that exposes the attorney to discipline or sanctions.

As a pleading, the complaint must conform to the applicable pleading standard imposed for that court. Historically, many courts required "fact pleading." Under this standard, the plaintiff must expressly state all the essential facts that support a claim, providing detailed information about the events and circumstances that form the basis of a legal action, rather than just giving general notice of the claim. As you can imagine, early in the litigation process, this can be quite challenging. Think about what you currently know about the November 10, Y-2 crash. There are many details you still need to learn.

Luckily, most courts today, including federal courts applying the Federal Rules of Civil Procedure, require only "notice pleading." Under this standard, the plaintiff need only state a legal theory that entitles the plaintiff to relief and sufficient facts to demonstrate that the theory is plausible. As compared to the fact pleading standard, the notice pleading standard is more relaxed. It prioritizes informing the defendant about the nature of the lawsuit rather than requiring sufficient evidence to prove each claim.

This does not mean, however, that there are no requirements for a complaint or that threadbare legal conclusions are sufficient. Even under the more relaxed notice pleading standards, certain elements must be pleaded with some degree of specificity.

Under Rule 8(a) of the Federal Rules of Civil Procedure, any complaint must contain, at minimum, three things: (1) a short and plain statement of the grounds for the court's jurisdiction; (2) a short and plain statement of the claim showing that the pleader is entitled to relief; and (3) a demand for the relief sought, which may include relief in the alternative or different types of relief.

The most challenging of these three requirements is the requirement of a short and plain statement of the claim under Rule 8(a)(2). To meet this pleading requirement, the complaint must contain a concise explanation of the factual allegations that support the plaintiff's cause of action, presented in a clear and straightforward manner, demonstrating why the plaintiff should prevail under the facts and the law. The correct balance must be struck between having too little detail and too much.

Luckily, the United States Supreme Court has provided some guidance in two cases interpreting Rule 8, *Bell Atlantic Corp. v. Twombly* and *Ashcroft v. Iqbal*. The standard set forth by these two cases is often called the "Twiqbal" pleading standard. The Twiqbal pleading standard requires a plaintiff to plead facts that make each claim "plausible" on its face, meaning that the plaintiff must allege sufficient details to show each claim is more than just possible. The complaint must contain facts that plausibly support each claim, not just facts that could theoretically support each claim. Simply stating legal conclusions without supporting factual allegations is never sufficient.

Some allegations and claims must be pleaded with even more specificity than Rule 8 requires. For these claims, the complaint must meet the pleading standard in Rule 9. Under Rule 9, when alleging certain special matters like fraud, mistake, or conditions precedent to suit, the plaintiff must state the circumstances with particularity. This means for allegations of special matters, the plaintiff must not only meet the general pleading standards but must also provide detailed facts, like who committed fraud, how a mistake was made, or when a condition precedent occurred.

As plaintiff's counsel, you may find these pleading standards somewhat challenging. Take comfort in the fact that the same standards apply to all pleadings, including those filed by the defense (like answers and affirmative defenses).

Civil complaints have a specific format, which may vary somewhat depending on court rules and local practice. In federal court, the requirements are set forth in Rule 10. Generally, they begin with a case caption, including a place for the clerk to add a case number once one has been assigned. Complaints are pleaded in sequentially numbered paragraphs with each paragraph containing a single allegation. Headings can be used to organize the information. Rather than repeat allegations, they can be incorporated by reference. After laying out the basic facts, the complaint then contains claims or causes of action, directed to one or more defendant. At the end of the complaint there is a demand for relief, known as an *ad damnum* clause. Finally, the complaint contains a signature block from counsel that is compliant with Rule 11. In some courts, a signed verification, under oath is required.

Once the complaint is drafted, it must be filed and served on the defendant. Pursuant to Rule 4, a federal court complaint can be served by personal delivery, mail, or electronic means. Rule 4 lays out a variety of different service methods that can be used. It is critical to read the rule carefully and select a proper method—there are different ways to properly serve different defendants under different circumstances.

The methods for filing vary by court. Some courts accept filings in person, by mail, or electronically. Courts also require different form documents that must be filed simultaneously with the complaint and filing fees that must be paid. In federal court, most civil cases are filed electronically, which requires that the attorney have an account to access the court's electronic case management system.

EXERCISE 3: Π ONLY

The law that applies in an FTCA case is the law of the state where the act or omission occurred, including that state's choice-of-law rules. Under that applicable state law, the United States is liable in the same manner and to the same extent as a private individual under similar circumstances.

Assume that you have concluded Schott may state a claim against the United States for negligence, and that under the applicable state law the elements of a negligence claim are: (1) duty; (2) breach; (3) causation; and (4) damages.

Also assume that you have concluded that Schott's spouse, Casey Schott, also has a valid claim for loss of consortium (based on the fact that Skylar Schott's injuries now prevent Skylar Schott from performing household duties to the same extent as prior to the collision). Under the applicable state law, the elements of a loss of consortium claim are: (1) a valid marriage; (2) an injury to the spouse; and (3) a loss of the spouse's services caused by that injury.

- Plaintiff's counsel (Π): draft a complaint asserting both claims, as well as a cover letter demonstrating proper service of the complaint.

CHAPTER 4

MOTION TO DISMISS (DEFENSE COUNSEL ONLY)

A pre-answer motion to dismiss is a dispositive motion often filed by a defendant in lieu of filing a complaint. The purpose of a pre-answer motion to dismiss is to ask the court to dismiss the complaint and not let the matter proceed toward trial. The basis for a pre-answer motion to dismiss, also known as a Rule 12(b) motion, is that the plaintiff has failed to state a claim or failed to follow a procedural rule relative to its complaint filing.

The practicalities of litigation often require a defendant to file such a motion. Due to statute of limitations deadlines as well as complaint requirements, a plaintiff is expected to name all potential parties at the time of the filing of the original complaint. Often, named parties are not actually involved in the lawsuit or are entities which have no connection to the matter at issue. In those cases, defense attorneys for those named, uninvolved parties may prepare and circulate a Stipulation of Discontinuance against those individuals or entities. This document essentially allows a named defendant to be removed from the case, and thus the caption. In addition, a complaint may be improperly filed or improperly prepared. For instance, all elements of a claim may not have been alleged within the complaint, or the complaint may have been improperly served. Under Federal Rule 12(b), there are enumerated reasons which serve as the basis for a motion to dismiss.

After filing a motion to dismiss, a plaintiff may oppose the motion. The court, upon review, may deny the motion and allow the case to proceed or grant the motion, with or without leave to file an amended complaint. The existence of the motion to dismiss within litigation calls for cautious drafting and thorough investigation as complaints are drawn and filed.

EXERCISE 4: Δ ONLY

A spouse can bring a loss of consortium claim under the FTCA, meaning that a spouse can sue the federal government for damages if the other spouse was injured due to the negligence of a federal employee. Both spouses must exhaust administrative remedies before suit, meaning that both spouses must tender an administrative claim to the agency within two years of the alleged tort. If only one spouse tenders such a claim within the time period, the other spouse's claim is forever barred.

Based upon your review of the administrative case file, Skylar Schott properly tendered an administrative claim to the USPS, but that claim made no mention of Schott's spouse, Casey Schott. Nor did Casey Schott tender a separate administrative claim. As a result, Casey Schott's loss of consortium claim is subject to dismissal under Rule 12.

- Defense counsel (Δ): Draft an appropriate motion package seeking dismissal under Rule 12.

CHAPTER 5

ANSWER (DEFENSE COUNSEL ONLY)

An answer is a written document filed by a defendant in a civil case. It has three primary functions. First, it is the defendant's opportunity to respond to the allegations in the complaint. Second, it is the defendant's opportunity to plead affirmative defenses, independent reasons why the defendant should prevail even if the plaintiff proves its claims. Third, it is the defendant's opportunity to add additional causes of action, including counterclaims, cross-claims, and third-party claims. Once an answer has been filed to all complaints, the pleadings are closed.

The first part of the answer is set forth in numbered paragraphs that align with the numbering in the complaint. In paragraph 1 of the answer, the defendant responds to the allegations in paragraph 1 of the complaint, and so on.

Under Rule 8(b), the defendant has three options when responding to the allegations in the complaint. The defendant can admit an allegation, deny an allegation, or profess a lack of information sufficient to respond to an allegation (which serves as a denial on that basis). General denials are not permitted; if the defendant intends to deny an allegation it must explain the factual or legal basis for that denial. The same pleading standards in Rules 8 and 9 that apply to the complaint also apply to the answer.

In its answer, the defendant must respond to all allegations in the complaint. The responses must be provided in good faith, meaning that the defendant must admit any allegations that it knows to be true, even if that is prejudicial to the defendant's case. If there is more than one allegation in a paragraph, the defendant must clarify which responses correspond to which allegation. Any allegations to which the defendant fails to respond are deemed to be admitted.

Once the defendant has responded to the allegations in the complaint, it can then set forth any affirmative defenses. Each defense is individually numbered. Under Rule 12, certain defenses are waived if they are not raised in the first instance. As a result, if the defendant intends to argue lack of personal jurisdiction, improper venue, insufficient process, or insufficient service of process, it must do so in either its answer or preliminary motion, whichever is filed first.

Other defenses, like lack of subject matter jurisdiction, failure to state a claim, and failure to join a party, can be raised later. However, most defendants will include these defenses, as well as any other applicable defenses, in the answer. Some affirmative defenses are listed in Rule 8(c). In addition, statutes, caselaw, and other legal authority can provide additional defenses. Any defenses pleaded must meet the pleading standard. You also must have a good faith basis for any defenses pleaded, to comply with Rule 11.

Counter claims, cross-claims, and third-party claims follow the pleading requirements of complaints. That is, in essence, what these claims are—a vehicle for the defendant to serve claims of its own against other parties or nonparties.

In most jurisdictions, a defendant must file an answer within a specific timeframe after being served with the complaint. Under Rule 12(a) of the Federal Rules of Civil Procedure, the defendant must respond to the complaint within 21 days of service unless service was timely waived or the defendant is the United States, in which case the answer must be filed within 60 days.

The format of an answer is quite similar to that of a complaint. It begins with a case caption, followed by responses in numbered paragraphs. The same headings as are used in the complaint are provided in the answer, to make the answer easier to align with the complaint. After responding to the allegations in the complaint, the defendant pleads its numbered affirmative defenses, followed by any additional claims. The answer contains a signature block and (in some cases) a verification.

The answer is filed and served on all parties or their counsel. Unlike the complaint, which must be served in strict accordance with Rule 4, answers and all other filings can generally be served through more informal means.

EXERCISE 5: Δ ONLY

Your motion to dismiss has been granted, leaving only Schott's negligence claim in the complaint.

- Defense counsel (Δ): Draft an answer to the complaint, asserting any affirmative defenses that are appropriate under Rule 11, given the informal fact discovery you've engaged in, to date. Among other defenses, ensure you plead a failure to state a claim.

CHAPTER 6

MOTION TO STRIKE (PLAINTIFF'S COUNSEL ONLY)

A motion to strike is a request made by one party to the judge asking the judge to remove a specific part of a pleading. It can be filed by either the plaintiff or the defendant. Pursuant to Federal Rule of Civil Procedure 12(f), the court may strike from a plaintiff either an insufficient defense or any redundant, immaterial, impertinent, or scandalous matter.

A motion to strike an insufficient defense set forth in the answer must be filed within 21 days after service of that answer. A motion to strike requires the same sort of accompanying documents as other preliminary motions, including a proposed order, the motion itself that cites Rule 12(f), a brief or memorandum of law in support, and a certificate of service.

EXERCISE 6: Π ONLY

Among other affirmative defenses, the United States has pleaded that the complaint fails to state a claim upon which relief may be granted. You believe the complaint adequately states a claim for negligence and that this affirmative defense should be stricken under Rule 12.

- Plaintiff's counsel (Π): Draft an appropriate motion package seeking dismissal under Rule 12.

CHAPTER 7

PROOF CHART

Case analysis is a critical step in developing litigation strategy. A strategic attorney will periodically evaluate the law and facts throughout the pretrial process. As information is gathered, the attorney will evaluate the strengths and weaknesses of the case.

A proof chart is one tool litigators use for organizing information about the case in a way that will be useful as they litigate. It is a document, often set up as a table, in which the attorney outlines the key elements of a legal claim or defense. Throughout discovery, the attorney populates the chart with citations to all sources of information that have been gathered that would support each element. These sources can include testimony and exhibits.

Throughout the discovery process, the attorney returns to the proof chart—revising it as the claims and defenses narrow and as information is gathered. If the tool is used consistently, it guides the attorney in determining what additional facts must be collected. Once discovery is completed, the attorney can use the proof chart to draft a dispositive motion or to prepare for trial.

EXERCISE 7: Π AND Δ

Draft a proof chart for use during discovery in the case. Make sure your chart covers not only the elements of the plaintiff's *prima facie* case but also the elements of any of the defendant's affirmative defenses.

CHAPTER 8

WITNESS INTERVIEW

Witness interviews play a large role in the investigation of any matter. Investigators play a primary role in securing and taking witness statements. Often, witnesses are listed in a police report or were present at the time of an incident. Witness testimony and statements can support claims or demonstrate failure to establish claims. Investigations are ongoing, and therefore the need for witness interviews is an important consideration throughout the investigation process.

A key consideration is *who* to interview. This question often answers itself, through documents and parties. Names may be added through the course of investigation and later discovery, and names may be removed from the list of potential witnesses as new information is gathered. Witnesses are people with lives and demands, and therefore investigators often do not work under perfect circumstances. Investigators need to coordinate with witnesses and entities to get the information they need.

As for the actual interview, witnesses should receive some instruction at the beginning of the interview and an explanation as to why they are being interviewed. The explanation can range from a very generic "information-gathering" description to a particular description of the issue being investigated. The witness should also understand the confidential nature of the investigation process, so that they are comfortable sharing information. This process is akin to an attorney explaining the concept of privilege to a client to facilitate the free flow of information between them.

Given the significance of witness interviews and the need to focus on the questions (and answers) provided, it is a good idea to have a separate notetaker (or notetaking process) involved in recording the information. This allows the investigator to focus on speaking with the witness and may assist with the free flow of communication between them.

EXERCISE 8: Π AND Δ

You have scheduled a meeting with a third-party witness who is willing to meet with you to discuss what they know about the case. Plaintiff's counsel will meet with Sydney David, Schott's primary care physician. Defense counsel will meet with Pat Swalsky, the police officer who arrived at the scene following the accident. You do not represent either of these parties, and you want to ensure they understand your role in the litigation.

Develop a plan for this interview, considering what information each witness may have that would help you litigate your case. Your discussions will not be subject to attorney-client privilege, so consider the fact that opposing counsel may seek to question this witness and may be entitled to inquire into the scope of your discussion.

a) Draft a written outline for the interview.
   - Plaintiff's counsel (Π), draft an outline for an interview of David.
   - Defense counsel (Δ), draft an outline for an interview of Swalsky.

b) Conduct the interview.
   - Plaintiff's counsel (Π), interview David.
   - Defense counsel (Δ), interview Swalsky.

CHAPTER 9

INITIAL DISCLOSURES

Initial disclosures are a set of documents and information that parties in a civil action must exchange at the outset of a case. The court need not order production, nor need any party request it. The rules require this information be disclosed without any order or request.

Rule 26(a)(1) of the Federal Rules of Civil Procedure outlines four categories of disclosures which must be made within 14 days of the initial case conference (unless the judge sets a different deadline by court order). The categories are as follows:

(i) the name and, if known, the address and telephone number of each individual likely to have discoverable information—along with the subjects of that information—that the disclosing party may use to support its claims or defenses, unless the use would be solely for impeachment;

(ii) a copy—or a description by category and location—of all documents, electronically stored information, and tangible things that the disclosing party has in its possession, custody, or control and may use to support its claims or defenses, unless the use would be solely for impeachment;

(iii) a computation of each category of damages claimed by the disclosing party—who must also make available for inspection and copying as under Rule 34 the documents or other evidentiary material, unless privileged or protected from disclosure, on which each computation is based, including materials bearing on the nature and extent of injuries suffered; and

(iv) for inspection and copying as under Rule 34, any insurance agreement under which an insurance business may be liable to satisfy all or part of a possible judgment in the action or to indemnify or reimburse for payments made to satisfy the judgment.

Initial disclosures require the parties to exchange basic information necessary to prepare for trial or settlement in any civil action before they engage in additional discovery that might be more tailored to the specific issues in the case.

EXERCISE 9: Π AND Δ

Draft a set of initial disclosures compliant with Rule 26(a)(1).

- Plaintiff's counsel (Π), direct your initial disclosures to Royal.
- Defense counsel (Δ), direct your initial disclosures to Schott.

CHAPTER 10

MEET AND CONFER

Discovery in a civil case is largely left up to the parties, with the court responsible for ensuring docket management and deciding any disputes raised by the parties. To enable the court to properly manage the case, and to ensure the parties have a reasonable plan for discovery, Federal Rule of Civil Procedure 16 requires that the court schedule a pretrial conference. During this conference, the court will set the ground rules for the litigation.

To aid the court in setting appropriate ground rules, Rule 26(f) requires the parties, through their counsel, meet and confer in advance of this conference. In specific, the parties must confer as soon as practicable and at least 21 days before the scheduling conference or a scheduling order is due. Thereafter, they must provide a status report to the judge. Some judges require the use of a specific form, while others leave the format to the discretion of counsel.

The rule does not require an in-person meeting, and it is common for the meeting to be held over the phone or through an online conferencing platform. One participating counsel must assume the responsibility of taking notes and providing the written report to the court.

The meet and confer has four primary purposes. First, the meet and confer guides the parties in planning discovery. Rule 26(f) requires that the parties discuss the scope, timing, and methods of discovery, including electronically stored information (ESI). The judge can use the information used as part of this discussion to set a discovery schedule that is realistic and tailored to the needs of the case.

Second, the meet and confer helps resolve issues early. Rule 26(f) requires the parties each think about their respective case and any potential discovery issues that may arise. The parties can then try to bypass these issues from occurring. If they cannot, the judge is on notice of the issues and can try to resolve them.

Third, the meet and confer is an early opportunity to discuss settlement. During the meet and confer, the parties may explore the possibility of resolving the case without full litigation. Rule 26(f) does not require the parties to come to the meet and confer session prepared for a full-fledged settlement negotiation, but it does require that the parties consider when they might be ready for such a negotiation. The judge can then schedule mediation with a magistrate judge or other neutral mediator.

Fourth, the meet and confer requires the parties consider issues of privilege and confidentiality before any discovery commences. The parties must establish protocols for handling this sensitive information.

If a party fails to participate in good faith with the meet and confer requirement, the court may impose sanctions. These sanctions including limitations on discovery or an award of attorney's fees.

EXERCISE 10: Π AND Δ

You must schedule a time to meet and confer with opposing counsel to develop a discovery plan under Rule 26(f).

a) Engage in the required discussion.
b) Complete the provided report form.

[CASE CAPTION]

JOINT RULE 26(f) REPORT

In accordance with Federal Rule of Civil Procedure 26(f), counsel for the parties conferred on (date) and submit the following report of their meeting for the court's consideration:

I. Counsel

A. Lead counsel for Plaintiff(s): ____________________

B. Lead counsel for Defendant(s): ____________________

C. Counsel who participated in Rule 26(f) conference on behalf of Plaintiff(s):

____

____

____

D. Counsel who participated in Rule 26(f) conference on behalf of Defendant(s):

____

____

____

II. Description of Claims and Defenses

The Parties should assume that the Court has read the Complaint and is familiar with the claims. However, the facts supporting those claims and defenses are unknown. Therefore, counsel shall summarize the primary facts that the parties contend support their claims and defenses and the threshold legal issues. **Counsel should not merely parrot their pleadings.** In addition, the Parties should attach critical documents to this report for the Court to review, if not attached to the pleadings already (e.g., in a contract case, the document(s) comprising the contract; in a personal injury case, photographs of the scene, etc.).

III. Stipulated Facts

The Parties **must stipulate to facts that are not in dispute**. In the interest of judicial economy and avoiding duplicative and/or unnecessary discovery, the Parties are required to identify and sign a stipulation outlining facts which they do not intend to dispute, although they are not required to identify disputed facts at this early stage.

IV. Jurisdiction

The Parties must state the basis for this Court's subject matter jurisdiction over the dispute.

V. Insurance Coverage and Deductibles

The Parties must disclose any insurance coverage and the cost of the retainer or deductible as required by Rule 26(a)(1)(A).

VI. Dispositive Motions

The Parties must identify if either side expects to file a case-dispositive motions, what motion, and approximate timeline for the motion.

VII. Anticipated Scope of Discovery

A. Summarize with specificity those issues on which the Parties will need to conduct discovery. Identify categories of information each Party needs in discovery and why.

B. Anticipated number of interrogatories per Party: ________________

C. Anticipated number of depositions per Party: ________________

D. To the extent either Party proposes to exceed the presumptive limits in the Federal Rules of Civil Procedure for discovery, explain the basis for that proposal.

E. Do the Parties anticipate the need for any third-party discovery? If so, identify the likely third parties and the discovery to be sought.

F. Do the Parties anticipate the need for experts? If so, identify the subjects on which the expert(s) may opine.

VIII. Status of Discovery

The Parties must summarize the status of discovery to-date. State the parties' agreement on timing, form and scope of informal disclosures. Specifically identify not only the information listed in Rule 26(a)(1), but any additional information the parties agree to disclose informally. If nothing has been done in terms of discovery, the Parties should explain why. Keep in mind that self-executing discovery must not be delayed until the pretrial conference.

IX. Proposed Case Management Deadlines

When completing this section, the Parties should presume that the Court **will** not **bifurcate fact and expert discovery**. Therefore, the Parties should propose dates that take that presumption into account.

A. Deadline to serve initial disclosures under Rule 26(a)(1) (*must be exchanged at least one (1) business day before Rule 16 conference):

____

B. Deadline to amend pleadings to add claims or Parties (*must be as early as practicable to avoid prejudice or unnecessary delays):

____

C. Deadline for affirmative expert reports (if any) and disclosure of lay witness opinion testimony with related information and documents (if any): ________________

D. Deadline for rebuttal expert reports (if any): ________________

E. Deadline to complete **all** discovery (fact and expert, including expert depositions): ____________________

F. If any Party seeks more than 120 days for discovery, explain why.

G. Deadline to file motion for summary judgment: ____________________

H. Estimated trial ready date: ____________________

I. Estimated Number of Days for Trial: ____________________

X. Deposition Scheduling

The Court expects the Parties to meet and confer as soon as practicable to set aside dates to hold open for depositions before the close of discovery. If the Parties have not already done so, the Court will order the Parties to do so within two weeks of the Rule 16 conference.

Have the Parties set aside dates for deposition? ___ Yes ___ No

If yes, what are those dates? ____________________

If no, when do the parties intend to confer, and how many dates do they intend to set aside?

____

XI. Electronic Discovery

Prior to the Rule 16 conference, the Court expects the Parties to have a thorough discussion about electronic discovery, including but not limited to 1) the need for electronically stored information (ESI), 2) sources of ESI, 3) the anticipated scope of electronic discovery, 4) the identity of potential custodians, 5) whether search terms will be necessary and, if so, any limitations thereto, 6) the respective burdens of collecting, reviewing, and producing ESI, including any claims for cost-shifting under the Federal Rules of Civil Procedure, and 7) any anticipated problems with electronic discovery. The Parties should summarize their discussion on these issues here. The Court expects counsel who attend the Rule 16 conference to be familiar with and able to discuss any ESI-related issues that might arise.

In addition, the Parties should state whether they have agreed to an ESI stipulation. If so, **the Parties should submit the stipulation to the Court in advance of the Rule 16 conference**. If not, the Parties should identify what issues need to be resolved to finalize the stipulation.

XII. Protective Orders and Confidentiality Agreements

The Parties should indicate whether they anticipate the need for a protective order in this case. If so, the Parties must explain what type of information needs protection from disclosure and why such protection is warranted under governing standards.

XIII. Alternative Dispute Resolution

A. Have the Parties engaged in any settlement discussions? If so, set forth the status of those negotiations. If not, explain why not.

B. Have the Parties explored or considered other forms of alternative dispute resolution? If so, summarize those efforts. If not, state the Parties' positions with respect to ADR.

C. Identify the individual who will attend the Rule 16 conference who will have authority to discuss settlement.

XIV. Consent to Send Case to a Magistrate Judge

The Parties should indicate whether they consent to have a United States Magistrate Judge conduct any or all proceedings in this case, pursuant to 28 U.S.C. § 636(c).

XV. Other Matters

The Parties should identify any other issues that have not been addressed above but may require the Court's attention (e.g., anticipated motions, bifurcation, privilege issues, etc.).

ACKNOWLEDGEMENT OF RULE 26(F) MEETING AND THE ABOVE SUBMISSION TO THE COURT:

______________________________	______________________________
Name and contact information	Name and contact information

CHAPTER 11

RULE 16 SCHEDULING CONFERENCE

In the early stages of litigation, the judge presiding over a case will issue an order under Rule 16. This order essentially sets the schedule and deadlines for all pretrial activities in a civil case, including discovery deadlines, motion deadlines, and dates for pretrial conferences. The order establishes a structured timeline for a case, preventing delays and ensuring all parties are prepared for trial. It typically addresses topics including:

- Deadlines for completing discovery;
- Deadlines for filing motions;
- Dates for pre-trial conferences; and
- Limits on the number of interrogatories or depositions.

The judge issues the Rule 16 order after a scheduling conference where parties discuss the case and answer any questions the judge may have about the schedule. The purpose of the conference is to:

- Expedite the case;
- Establish early control;
- Discourage wasteful pretrial activities;
- Improve the quality of the trial; and
- Facilitate settlement.

Rule 16 governs the judge's authority to issue the scheduling order and the parties' appearance at the conference. The scheduling order limits the time to join parties, amend pleadings, complete discovery, and file motions.

The court must issue the scheduling order as soon as possible and within 90 days of the defendant being served with the complaint or 60 days after the defendant appears.

Attorneys should be proactive in preparing for and complying with the scheduling order, as these early stages can significantly impact the course of the litigation.

EXERCISE 11: Π AND Δ

The judge presiding over this case has ordered that you appear for a Rule 16 conference. Your client need not attend. You should be prepared to discuss any discovery issues or other matters you believe ought to be addressed by the court at this preliminary state of litigation.

a) Draft an outline for the anticipated discussion.
b) Engage in the conference, discussing all necessary points.

CHAPTER 12

SERVING INTERROGATORIES AND DOCUMENT REQUESTS

The discovery process is more than just an exchange of information between the parties. Discovery is an opportunity for you as the attorney to determine the strength and weakness of your case and of your opponent's. With this goal in mind, you can approach the discovery process to obtain the information you may need to support your position in a summary judgment motion following conclusion of discovery, support your valuation of the case during a pretrial settlement conference, or succeed at trial.

The federal rules allow for multiple avenues by which to obtain information. Interrogatories and requests to produce documents serve as two main avenues of discovery exchange. When drafting these types of documents, consider specific demands which would lead to information which is likely to support claims or defenses. These considerations would form the basis of the specific demands or interrogatories. Consider also structuring interrogatories or document requests within reasonable boundaries, such as time limitations or other narrowing factors, or adding defined terms for clarity amongst the parties. From a structural standpoint, a typical interrogatory document or document request contains these key parts: instructions, definitions, and specific questions/demands.

Let's first consider interrogatories. Interrogatories are prepared questions which must be answered under oath. Federal Rule of Civil Procedure 33 governs "Interrogatories to Parties." In federal practice, only 25 interrogatories may be demanded, unless a party moves the court to grant leave to serve additional demands. The breadth of information which may be demanded is quite broad and only needs to relate to any matter which may fall under Rule 26(b). The party served with interrogatories must complete them within 30 days. Keep in mind, local rules may factor in this process. The key to responding to interrogatories properly is to treat each question individually and provide a specific response. Any objections in lieu of an answer must be stated with specificity—recall, the purpose of discovery is to effectuate an *efficient* resolution. When drafting interrogatories, the document often contains instructions, definitions, and specific interrogatories.

Document requests are another avenue of discoverable information. Rule 34 governs this mode of discovery. As provided within that rule, document requests must be prepared within the scope of Rule 26(b). For example, documents such as photographs or writings may be demanded, and permission to inspect property may also be demanded. Document requests are used to obtain both helpful information and perhaps information that is harmful to a case or claim. Doing so allows the parties to see clearly the strengths and weaknesses of the case, and therefore, be able to choose the best course toward resolution. When drafting document requests, the document often contains instructions, definitions, and specific demands. Parties receiving a document request must either raise specific objections or produce the documents. Typically, a combination is used, wherein the responding party provides a written response containing objections and noting the specific documents which will be produced.

Keep in mind that the discovery process assumes that counsel will work together to amicably exchange information and efficiently arrive at case resolution. In practice, judges prefer not to be involved in discovery disputes, and it is therefore incumbent on counsel to keep the discovery process moving forward and communicate issues for self-contained resolution.

EXERCISE 12: Π AND Δ

Draft a set of 20 interrogatories and 20 document requests to be served on the opposing party. Ensure your requests are compliant with the discovery limitations in Rule 26(b).

- Plaintiff's counsel (Π), direct your interrogatories and document requests to Royal.
- Defense counsel (Δ), direct your interrogatories and document requests to Schott.

CHAPTER 13

RESPONDING TO INTERROGATORIES AND DOCUMENT REQUESTS

In most civil litigation, the parties engage in "paper discovery," including interrogatories and document requests. Once these requests have been properly served, the receiving party must respond in accordance with Federal Rules of Civil Procedure 33 and 34.

The first step is always to carefully review the interrogatories and requests. Ensure they comply with the limits set forth in the Rules or the discovery order governing the case. Remember that Rule 33 only permits 25 interrogatories, including subparts, without leave of court. If discovery is overly burdensome, then attempt to negotiate with opposing counsel as to the breadth or depth of demands.

Next determine if any interrogatories or requests are substantively objectionable based on scope, relevance, or privilege. Remember that the scope of discovery, which is set by Rule 26, is much broader than the scope of what is admissible at trial.

After reviewing the interrogatories and requests, you can begin collecting documents and drafting responses. In your responses, object only to portions of any interrogatory or request that are truly objectionable. Provide compete and truthful substantive responses to the remainder. Proper objections include that the interrogatory or request:

- Is overly broad or unduly burdensome;
- Calls for privileged information (attorney-client, work product); or
- Seeks information outside the party's possession, custody, or control.

Many common objections to admissibility, like "relevance" or "hearsay" are inappropriate at the discovery state of litigation. Objections must be specific; the Federal Rules do not permit broad, blanket objections. Vague objections may be overruled. Use a privilege log if withholding documents.

A substantive response to interrogatories may be written, or, in the alternative, the responding party can direct the propounding party to a document where the substantive response can be located. Substantive responses to interrogatories must be verified under oath.

Documents produced must either be organized by request, or documents may be produced as they are kept in the ordinary course.

Discovery responses are due within 30 days unless extended by agreement or court order. Be timely—courts can impose sanctions for late responses.

EXERCISE 13: Π AND Δ

Draft your client's objections and responses to the interrogatories and documents requests served by the opposing party. Ensure your objections and responses are compliant with Rule 12(g).

- Plaintiff's counsel (Π), respond to the interrogatories and document requests served by Royal.
- Defense counsel (Δ), respond to the interrogatories and document requests served by Schott.

CHAPTER 14

NOTICING A FACT WITNESS DEPOSITION

At some point during the discovery process, it often becomes clear that testimony will be relevant to the dispute. The Federal Rules of Civil Procedure allow the parties to use the deposition process to formally gather that testimony during the discovery phase of litigation. This prevents trial by ambush. When used properly, depositions allow the parties to anticipate and prepare for trial testimony.

A deposition is a formal legal proceeding in which a witness or party to a lawsuit gives sworn testimony outside of court, usually as part of the discovery process in a civil case. The witness or party is referred to as the "deponent." The deponent's testimony is recorded by a court reporter and may, under certain circumstances, be used in support of a motion or offered into evidence at trial.

Although a deposition typically takes place in a law office, conference room, or remotely via video, the testimony given is under oath and is treated as seriously as if it was given at a hearing or trial. Attorneys for all involved parties may participate and ask questions. Generally, a transcript is created and can be used in court if the deponent is unavailable to testify or if the deponent is a trial witness and contradicts prior deposition testimony on the witness stand.

The litigant who wants to question a deponent must provide proper notice of the deposition to the deponent and all other involved parties. This is a multi-step process.

The first step is to determine which deponents should be questioned. Although the Federal Rules of Civil Procedure do not so require, it is common courtesy to contact that deponent or the deponent's counsel to discuss scheduling and find a mutually agreeable date and time. If the deponent is a party to the case, notice must then be provided pursuant to Rule 30(b)(1). If the deponent is a non-party, the deponent must be served with a subpoena pursuant to Rule 45.

Under Rule 30(b)(1), the deposition notice must include:

- The deponent's name and address (or, if unknown, a description to identify them);
- The date, time, and location of the deposition;
- The method of recording (e.g., stenographic, audiovisual, or both).

If the deposition is to be conducted remotely, the notice must also state so specifically.

The Federal Rules do not specify an exact timeframe for noticing a deposition, but reasonable notice is required. Local rules or case-specific scheduling orders may impose a specific deadline.

If the deponent is a non-party, notice must be provided in the form of a subpoena under Rule 45. Rule 45 requires similar information as is required under Rule 30.

Some courts may require the notice or subpoena to be filed with the court. Most courts have no such requirement.

Once the deposition is properly noticed, the litigant taking the deposition must ensure a court reporter and/or videographer has been hired. The litigant must ensure that a remote platform or conference room is arranged. Then the litigant noticing the deposition must prepare to question the deponent.

EXERCISE 14: Π AND Δ

You have elected to depose the opposing party and one key fact witness in the case. Plaintiff's counsel will depose Royal and Swalsky. Defense counsel will depose Schott and David. Note that Swalsky and David are third parties who are unrepresented in this litigation. For each third-party deponent, ensure you request that the deponent produce relevant documents at the time of the deposition (and describe those documents in the notice). Draft a deposition notice and, as applicable, a subpoena, as well as a cover letter properly serving the notice.

- Plaintiff's counsel (Π), draft deposition notices/subpoenas for depositions of Royal and Swalsky.
- Defense counsel (Δ), draft deposition notices/subpoenas for depositions of Schott and David.

CHAPTER 15

PREPARING TO DEFEND A FACT WITNESS DEPOSITION

Preparing to defend a deposition begins when you first meet your client. It is important to explain the litigation process, including the fact that there will be a time when he or she will have to testify at a deposition. Plan on meeting with your witness in person, at least on one occasion, in preparation for the deposition. Depending on the complexity of the case and the witness's familiarity with the process, additional sessions may be necessary. Aside from understanding the process, certain instructions are key for your witness to hear and apply.

For any witness, the center focus of the deposition should be to speak the truth. It is incumbent upon you, the attorney, to explain and reiterate this to your witness. Recall, at the end of the day, you are an officer of the court, and the intention of any deposition is to extract the truth for purposes of case resolution. That said, the goal is to have every witness speak the truth—even if it is detrimental to your case. Why? Because it is better to know the facts and deal with them than to prepare a case for trial on falsities.

In addition to truth-telling, it is within the realm of reason to counsel a witness to answer only the question asked. Doing so helps the witness to *listen* to the question and answer it, rather than sharing unlimited information. Essentially, remind the witness that the attorney asking the questions has the burden of asking the questions. Make the attorney work for his or her answers. Additionally, it is within the realm of reason to counsel a client to ask for clarification if a question is not understood. In that instance, the attorney will either repeat the question, rephrase the question, or request the stenographer to read back that portion of the transcript containing the question.

Document review in advance of a deposition may be helpful to a plaintiff to refamiliarize himself or herself with the incident and/or claims. However, be aware that the deposing attorney will likely ask the witness whether he or she reviewed any documents in advance of the deposition. Therefore, consider whether an advanced review will benefit your client or not. Some details may be difficult to remember, with or without a document review. It is important to counsel your witness as to providing estimates or ranges when dealing with numbers, years, distances, and the like. Doing so allows for a qualified response, and the ability for the attorney to argue within a range.

Defense of a deposition involves listening. Listening to the questions asked, the form in which they are asked, the answers given, and the potential for any areas of protected information or privilege. Valid objections include form of the question if compound, ambiguous, or repetitious, for instance; privilege, if the question imposes on this right; and relevancy, if the question is off-topic. Usually, counsel will be professional during the course of a deposition and not attempt to ask a question which would raise a privilege concern. However, on occasion, an attorney may be difficult or unprofessional during a deposition. Often, ignoring such behavior may cure the issue. If not, a judge may be called during a deposition or a motion to regulate behavior may be made to provide relief.

EXERCISE 15: Π AND Δ

You have received a notice of deposition for your client. Meet with your client to prepare your client (either Schott or Royal) to be deposed.

a) Draft an outline of topics to discuss, including any exhibits you wish to review.
   - Plaintiff's counsel (Π), create an outline to be used in preparing Schott to be deposed.
   - Defense counsel (Δ), create an outline to be used in preparing Royal to be deposed.

b) Conduct the preparation session.
   - Plaintiff's counsel (Π), prepare Schott.
   - Defense counsel (Δ), prepare Royal.

CHAPTER 16

TAKING A FACT WITNESS DEPOSITION

Taking an effective fact witness deposition requires significant preparation in advance. The first step of your preparation is to determine the goal of the deposition. Consider whether you need to gather information, confirm information you already know or believe you know, or develop a record for motion practice. Often you will have multiple different goals, and these goals will help determine how you question the deponent.

The second step of your preparation is to gather as much information as you can in advance of the deposition. Review the pleadings, discovery responses, prior witness statements, and documents. Investigate the deponent's background, including the deponent's employment history, affiliations, and potential biases.

The third step of your preparation is to plan your questioning strategy. Most attorneys draft an outline, but it is dangerous to fully draft questions in advance. An effective deposition requires that the questioning attorney listen to the deponent's answer and follow up or adjust questioning in accordance with the answers given. This can be difficult to do if you have written a list of questions. A better strategy is to outline a list of topics, leaving space in your outline to take notes and write potential questions as the deposition unfolds.

If you plan to show the deponent exhibits during the deposition, you will need sufficient copies for the deponent, the court reporter, and all participating parties or attorneys. In some jurisdictions, attorneys pre-mark the exhibits by letter or number. In other jurisdictions, the court reporter will mark exhibits during the deposition.

Once everyone has assembled, you should begin the deposition with opening formalities. Introduce yourself and state who you represent on the record.

Next, discuss and agree with counsel about the ground rules for the objections. A good practice is to agree that the deposition be taken pursuant to the Federal Rules of Civil Procedure. Under the Federal Rule 30(c)(2), objections must be stated concisely and in a non-argumentative manner, all objections other than those to form are reserved for trial, and the only valid reasons for instructing a witness not to answer are privilege, court order, or to stop harassment. Pursuant to Rule 30(e), if requested during the deposition, the deponent has 30 days to review the transcript and note any errors.

With these formalities out of the way, you can then ask the court reporter to swear in the deponent. Typically, you then provide instructions to the deponent. These can include instructions on how to handle confusing questions or the need to take breaks.

Once the deponent understands the process, you can begin the substantive questioning. Although you need not do so, the typical practice is to begin with background questions. When questioning, most attorneys cast a wide net, gathering information through open-ended questions before drilling down into details using leading questions. Questioning tends to focus on material issues in the case that cannot be explored fully through paper discovery.

At the conclusion of your questioning, other the other parties and counsel will have an opportunity to question the deponent. Once all the questioning is complete, arrangements should be made to order copies of the transcript from the court reporter.

EXERCISE 16: Π AND Δ

You have elected to depose the opposing party. Plaintiff's counsel will depose Royal. Defense counsel will depose Schott. Prepare a deposition outline and any applicable exhibits for the deposition, which you will be responsible for conducting. Opposing counsel will defend during the deposition.

a) Draft a deposition outline.
   - Plaintiff's counsel (Π), create an outline to use for questioning Royal.
   - Defense counsel (Δ), create an outline to use for questioning Schott.

b) Question the deponent during the deposition.
   - Plaintiff's counsel (Π), question Royal.
   - Defense counsel (Δ), question Schott.

CHAPTER 17

MOTION TO COMPEL

A motion to compel is a request for the court to order compliance with discovery obligations under the Federal Rules of Civil Procedure. It is typically filed following a failure to respond to discovery entirely or a discovery response that is incomplete or evasive. Motions to compel are primarily governed by Rules 30, 33, 34, 36, and 37 of the Federal Rules. Different rules apply depending on the circumstances.

For example, if the defendant properly serves interrogatories and the plaintiff refuses to answer, claiming the questions are overbroad and unduly burdensome, the defendant can file a motion to compel under Rule 37(a)(3)(B)(iii), arguing that the interrogatories seek relevant and proportional information within the scope of Rule 26(b)(1).

If a plaintiff serves a subpoena seeking the appearance of a third-party deponent and that deponent fails to appear, the plaintiff can file a motion to compel under Rule 37(d)(1)(A)(i), seeking sanctions and an order compelling the witness to attend. The court can hold the deponent in contempt under Rule 45(g).

Before a motion can be filed, there must be an attempt to resolve the dispute informally. Rule 37(a)(1) requires the involved parties to a discovery dispute confer in good faith before a motion to compel is filed. These efforts should be documented, because they will be included as part of the motion package if efforts to resolve the dispute fail.

If filed, the motion should explain what discovery was sought and why that discovery is within the bounds of Rule 26(b)(1). The motion should describe the alleged non-compliance by the opposing party or third party and detail efforts to resolve the discovery dispute without court intervention.

Motions to compel look similar to other motions, like motions to dismiss, with one exception. In addition to an order, motion, memorandum of law in support, and certificate of service, you must typically attach a certification outlining efforts to meet and confer to resolve the discovery dispute. As is often the case, there may be local rules and judge-specific policies that apply to your motion practice.

EXERCISE 17: Π AND Δ

Despite being properly noticed, the third party you noticed for a deposition (either Swalsky or David) refused to appear for a deposition. Neither has produced the documents you requested. Assume that you have twice contacted the third party by phone, once the day of the scheduled deposition and again a week later. The calls went directly to voicemail and were not returned.

It now appears that you must move to compel the third party's compliance with your discovery requests. Draft an appropriate motion package under Rule 37.

CHAPTER 18

DEPOSING AN ORGANIZATION

Federal Rule of Civil Procedure 30(b)(6) depositions were created to solve a major problem in litigation—the difficulty of obtaining reliable, binding testimony from organizations. Unlike individuals, a corporation or other entity cannot speak for itself, so Rule 30(b)(6) provides a way to depose a business, government agency, or other organization by requiring it to designate a representative to testify on the organization's behalf.

A deposition notice under Rule 30(b)(6) seeking the testimony of an organization has additional information that need not be included in a deposition notice seeking the testimony of an individual. In specific, the notice must describe with reasonable particularity the topics upon which the organization must present a designee or designees.

Rule 30(b)(6) was amended in December 2020 to include an explicit meet and confer requirement. This amendment requires the parties to confer in good faith about the deposition before it takes place, helping to avoid disputes and ensure clarity on the topics to be covered.

Once the topics have been agreed upon, the organization selects one or more designees to testify on its behalf. These designees must be thoroughly educated on the topics they will address, even if the person selected as a designee lacks personal knowledge. If necessary, the organization must review documents and interview employees to prepare the designee. A designee's testimony binds the organization—meaning the organization is responsible for the answers given.

The deposition itself is handled like any other deposition under Rule 30, with questioning by attorneys, objections, and a court reporter transcribing the proceeding. If a designee cannot answer basic questions on a properly noticed topic, the organization may face sanctions under Rule 37.

EXERCISE 18: Π AND Δ

Based on the discovery collected to date, you believe there may have been multiple prior car collisions in the same intersection where Schott and Royal had their accident. Wildcat City is responsible for maintaining the traffic lights and signs at that intersection and would possess information about prior collisions. Draft a notice of deposition directed to Wildcat City that is compliant with Rule 30(b)(6) as well as a cover letter demonstrating proper service of that notice.

CHAPTER 19

EXPERT DISCOVERY

Expert disclosures under Federal Rule 26 regard the requirement that parties to a lawsuit must disclose the identity of any expert witnesses they intend to use at trial, along with a detailed description of items such as their opinions, qualifications, and the basis for their expertise.

This information is typically prepared in the form of a report or summary. The timing of expert disclosures is important, depending on the complexity of the case and court orders, and they must be made before trial. Expert disclosures are prepared as either a "standard" expert report under Rule 26(a)(2)(B), which requires full disclosure for retained experts, or else a "summary" disclosure under Rule 26(a)(2)(C) for certain other witnesses. A careful reading of the rules is important to adherence to these disclosure requirements.

In practice, it is helpful to know who opposing counsel intends to name as an expert witness. Expert discovery assists the parties in developing trial strategy and provides a basis for impeachment if trial testimony differs from deposition testimony. Expert disclosure and expert opinions can lead to settlement discussions if information is learned that affects case valuation or negotiations. However, be aware that expert disclosure and the retention of experts is expensive and time-consuming. It can pose risks that involve testimony that is damaging to a party's case. Each case calls for an independent assessment as to whether expert disclosure and expert witnesses would be beneficial to the case.

EXERCISE 19: Π AND Δ

You have retained an expert witness to address the claim for lost wages in the case. Plaintiff's counsel has retained Ash Closius. Defense counsel has retained Chris Lore. Each expert has drafted an expert report and has provided this report and other supplemental information to each respective party. Prepare and serve expert disclosures consistent with Rule 26(a)(2) and serve them on opposing counsel.

- Plaintiff's counsel (Π), serve disclosures for Closius.
- Defense counsel (Δ), serve disclosures for Lore.

CHAPTER 20

EXPERT DEPOSITIONS

Expert depositions play an important role in the litigation process. Often, an attorney seeks to depose an expert to obtain testimony to use in support of a motion to exclude an expert or limit the expert's testimony. Or an attorney may seek expert testimony to show how the expert agrees with their position on the case. An attorney may also seek expert testimony to validate the opinions set forth in an expert report. Prior to taking an expert deposition, expert disclosures should have been made. To that end, there is knowledge on both sides as to the use of the expert and other details associated with expert disclosure. Here is where preparation begins.

When preparing for an expert deposition, it is best to begin by reviewing the expert report and any associated expert disclosures exchanged during the discovery process. Ultimately, remember that an expert witness is used to bolster claims and defenses. Understanding the opinions of the expert and how those opinions affect your position in the case can guide you through creating the proper questions to ask.

Federal Rule 26(a)(2)(B) outlines the scope of required disclosure of an expert report. In addition, Federal Rule of Evidence 702 governs expert testimony in legal proceedings. The rule establishes the qualifications of expert witnesses and the basis for their testimony. Recently, Rule 702 has been changed to include a standard of "more likely than not" to meet certain thresholds. The change to Rule 702 has the effect of guiding courts in evaluating the qualifications of expert witnesses. Specifically, thresholds include that the witness must be "qualified" as an expert by knowledge, skill, experience, training, or education; witness testimony must be based on sufficient facts or data; and witness testimony must be based on reliable principles and methods. The proponent of expert testimony holds the burden of establishing these criteria.

It is important to discuss these recent changes with an expert witness, so he/she is prepared to defend the principles and methods used as appropriate and reliable in a particular case. Doing so will ensure the strength of the testimony for use in motions and/or trial.

EXERCISE 20 : Π AND Δ

You have elected to depose the opposing party's expert witness. Plaintiff's counsel will depose Lore. Defense counsel will depose Closius. Prepare a deposition outline, and any applicable exhibits, for the deposition, which you will be responsible for conducting. Opposing counsel will defend during the deposition.

a) Draft a deposition outline, including reference to any exhibits.
   - Plaintiff's counsel (Π), draft an outline to use in questioning Lore.
   - Defense counsel (Δ), draft an outline to use in questioning Closius.

b) Conduct the deposition.
   - Plaintiff's counsel (Π), question Lore.
   - Defense counsel (Δ), question Closius.

CHAPTER 21

CLIENT COUNSELING

Client counseling is an art, and, as such, it is a skill that must be continuously developed through practice and tailored to suit the needs of each client. The foundation of client counseling involves providing options for a client as well as your professional recommendation. Client counseling is all about highlighting the potential risks and potential benefits associated with each potential decision. As an attorney, you are not just a "counselor" but an "educator." There is no room to sugarcoat the situation for your client. It is best practice to be straightforward and keep all facts in the light. Doing so will ensure your client has all the information at hand with which to determine the next best step along the litigation timeline.

Client counseling occurs throughout every stage of the litigation process. However, there are key points during the litigation process when client counseling skills are particularly important. For instance, before litigation begins, you will need to counsel your client about pre-suit options including early settlement or pressing forward into litigation. If the litigation process is underway, you will need to guide your client through phases of discovery and motion practice and ultimately counsel your client through the options of settlement or proceeding to trial.

During the litigation timeline, the power of decisions shifts between attorney and client. Generally, matters involving settlement rest in the hands of the client, while matters involving the litigation process rest in the hands of the attorney. For instance, in the pre-suit phase, the decision of whether to settle or sue a matter lies in the hands of a client. While in the litigation phase, the decision of whether to file a motion, raise a defense in a pleading, or depose a witness lies in the hands of the attorney. However, because of the at-will attorney-client relationship, an attorney can always close a matter if the decision contradicts the attorney's recommended course (and vice versa). To establish the attorney-client relationship and invoke the trust element, which is key to fostering that relationship, it is best practice to communicate to your client those key decisions relating to the litigation process itself.

Client counseling "styles" are often discussed in terms of a "spectrum," from client-centered counseling (left side of the spectrum) to collaborative counseling (middle of the spectrum) to attorney-centered counseling (right side of the spectrum). Depending on the type of decision being made and the client being counseled, an attorney may employ any one of these counseling styles at the time. For instance, if a client is new to the litigation process, and considering whether to sue a case, the attorney may employ the "attorney-centered" counseling style to take a more involved approach to guiding the client down the best path to resolution. That said, if the litigation proceeds, that same attorney may shift counseling styles to become more "collaborative" during the discovery phase. As the litigation proceeds and the client becomes more comfortable with the process, the same attorney may later employ a "client-centered" approach when handling settlement discussions with the client. The key to understanding and employing counseling styles is to keep your style malleable to fit the needs of the client and particular decision.

EXERCISE 21: Π AND Δ

Based on discovery, your understanding of the case has evolved since your initial meeting with your client. Prepare to meet with your client to provide an update, discuss the next steps, and counsel your client on the potential upsides and downsides of a settlement before trial.

a) Draft an outline for the counseling session.
   - Plaintiff's counsel (Π), draft an outline for your session with Schott.
   - Defense counsel (Δ), draft an outline for your session with Royal.
b) Conduct the counseling session.
   - Plaintiff's counsel (Π), counsel Schott.
   - Defense counsel (Δ), counsel Royal.

CHAPTER 22

MOTION FOR SUMMARY JUDGMENT

A motion for summary judgment is a key dispositive motion often brought following the close of all discovery. Essentially, pursuant to Rule 56 of the Federal Rules of Civil Procedure, a motion for summary judgment asks the court to decide the merits of the case on the law, in lieu of continued litigation and the need for trial. Given this request, the standard for a motion for summary judgment is demonstration of the absence of any genuine dispute of any "material fact" which would necessitate the need for a trial and jury decision. In practice, it makes sense that the time to file a motion for summary judgment ripens upon the close of discovery because at that time, there are no additional "facts" which may arise during written exchange of documents or oral depositions.

Preparing a motion for summary judgment begins all the way back in the early investigation of a case—not when discovery is completed—and the attorney takes a pen to paper. Why? Because from the early days of intake of a matter, it is important to consider the claims and legal theories upon which the case will be argued. "Frontloading" litigation in this regard allows an attorney to think through the necessary documents and information to demand within written discovery demands and prepare the necessary questions to ask during party and non-party depositions. Doing so creates a "record" which provides the documentary proof and testimony necessary to "demonstrate the absence of any question of fact" which requires a jury to decide.

The party bringing a motion for summary judgment is known as the "movant" or "moving party." The burden lies on the moving party to demonstrate that there is no issue of material fact necessitating trial, and therefore, the moving party is entitled to judgment as a matter of law. To do so, the moving party prepares motion papers, consisting of a notice of motion to the court with accompanying attorney affidavit and memorandum of law. Key to understanding these drafts is to continually refer to the standard. Doing so will help you pull the necessary facts from the file to argue your case.

The party responding to a motion for summary judgment is known as the "respondent" or "responding party." A response is known as the "opposition," and as noted, short timeframes apply. In responding to a motion for summary judgment, the respondent's goal is to demonstrate the failure of the moving party to establish the absence of a material fact, therefore necessitating trial. Often, opposition papers include not only an attorney affidavit in opposition to the motion, but also an accompanying expert affidavit. In practice, submitting an expert affidavit only invites the moving party to do the same in return, when preparing reply papers. Nonetheless, if submission results in a "battle of the experts," in which each party disagrees with the other's expert, then the opposition is successful in its attempt. A question of fact is likely raised, and the motion is likely to be denied.

Upon receipt of the opposition papers, the moving party has yet one more opportunity to file a response, termed "reply" papers. Within the reply papers, a moving party would clarify any arguments raised in opposition. Reply papers tend to be short and streamlined. Keep in mind the practicalities of motion practice—the courts are busy and motions tend to be voluminous.

There are timeframes for filing, responding, and replying to motions for summary judgment provided under the Federal Rules and corresponding state rules. In short, when filing this type of motion, be prepared for a short response time in reply. Also, when receiving a motion for summary judgment, be aware of the clock as time is limited. While motions may be heard during oral arguments, not all motions for summary judgment are heard. Therefore, legal writing skills are supremely important to achieving success in motion practice.

The court issues a Decision and Opinion following its review of the papers and hearing oral argument, if there are any. If the motion is denied, then the matter proceeds forward to pre-trial settlement and/or trial. Be aware that if settlement is pursued, the issues raised in the motion for summary judgment (and heard by the court) may affect case valuation and impact settlement figures, for good or bad. Like frontloading the early stages of a case, attorneys should thoughtfully consider whether to file a motion for summary judgment, as its outcome can have lasting effects on the matter. If the motion is granted, then the movant receives judgment as a matter of law and the matter is dismissed. A case dismissed by summary judgment is indicative of a case that should not have been sued in the first instance.

EXERCISE 22: Π AND Δ

Discovery has now closed. Based on that discovery, each party believes it may be entitled to partial summary judgment. Plaintiff's counsel believes it is entitled to summary judgment in its favor on duty and breach. Defense counsel believes it is entitled to summary judgment on causation and damages for Schott's personal injury claim. The applicable local rules state as follows:

> On motions for summary judgment, the movant shall furnish a statement which sets forth material facts as to which there does not exist a genuine issue, in separately numbered paragraphs citing to the affidavits and other

documents submitted in support of the motion. A motion for summary judgment unaccompanied by a statement of material facts not in dispute shall be dismissed. The opponent of summary judgment shall furnish, with its opposition papers, a responsive statement of material facts, addressing each paragraph of the movant's statement, indicating agreement or disagreement and, if not agreed, stating each material fact in dispute and citing to the affidavits and other documents submitted in connection with the motion; any material fact not disputed shall be deemed undisputed for purposes of the summary judgment motion. In addition, the opponent may also furnish a supplemental statement of disputed material facts, in separately numbered paragraphs citing the affidavits and other documents submitted in connection with the motion, if necessary to substantiate the factual basis for opposition. The movant shall respond to any such supplemental statement of disputed material facts as above, with its reply papers. Each statement of material facts shall be a separate document (not part of a brief) and shall not contain legal argument or conclusions of law.

Draft a motion package, seeking partial summary judgment as outlined above, that is compliant with Rule 56.

- Plaintiff's counsel (∏), move for summary judgment on the basis that there is no dispute of fact as to duty and breach such that you are entitled to judgment in your client's favor on these two elements of your *prima facie* case.
- Defense counsel (Δ), move for summary judgment on the basis that there is no dispute of fact as to causation and damages such that you are entitled to judgment in your client's favor on these two elements of the plaintiff's *prima facie* case.

CHAPTER 23

OPPOSING A MOTION

If the opposing party files a motion, you typically have the right to file an opposition explaining why the motion should be denied. Under Rule 6 of the Federal Rules of Civil Procedure, the default deadline for filing an opposition is 14 days after the motion is served unless the motion seeks summary judgment under Rule 56. In the case of a summary judgment motion, you have 21 days to file the opposition. Local rules and court orders may also impact these timeframes, so ensure you consult both before calculating your response date. If you need more time, you can file a motion for extension before the deadline expires.

The first step before filing an opposition is to read the motion carefully to understand the relief requested and the legal arguments made. Review the supporting memorandum, affidavits, and exhibits. Identify any weaknesses in the motion, such as: procedural defects (including missed deadlines and improper service), failure to meet the legal standard, and insufficient evidence. You should also determine whether you oppose the relief sought. If you do not, you need not file an opposition. Here, it is best practice to inform the court and counsel via letter that the motion is unopposed.

If, after review, you oppose the relief sought and you have identified a reason why the court should deny your opponent that relief, you should begin preparing the opposition. Research the law and gather evidence to support your argument.

After your research is complete, you are ready to draft your opposition package. Typically this includes a proposed order reflecting your belief as to what relief should be granted. Often this order simply suggests that the motion be denied, but sometimes additional nuance is required. You will also need to draft an opposition brief. In your brief, state the legal standard the court must apply; refute each argument made in the motion using legal authority and references to facts; and attach any declarations, affidavits, or other evidence as exhibits. Like other court filings, the brief should contain the case caption and your signature block.

Finally, draft a certificate of service. File the opposition brief and any supporting documents with the court before the deadline. Serve a copy on all parties.

EXERCISE 23: Π AND Δ

Opposing counsel has filed a motion for partial summary judgment. The applicable local rules state as follows:

> On motions for summary judgment, the movant shall furnish a statement which sets forth material facts as to which there does not exist a genuine issue, in separately numbered paragraphs citing to the affidavits and other documents submitted in support of the motion. A motion for summary judgment unaccompanied by a statement of material facts not in dispute shall be dismissed. The opponent of summary judgment shall furnish, with its opposition papers, a responsive statement of material facts, addressing each paragraph of the movant's statement, indicating agreement or disagreement and, if not agreed, stating each material fact in dispute and citing to the affidavits and other documents submitted in connection with the motion; any material fact not disputed shall be deemed undisputed for purposes of the summary judgment motion. In addition, the opponent may also furnish a supplemental statement of disputed material facts, in separately numbered paragraphs citing to the affidavits and other documents submitted in connection with the motion, if necessary to substantiate the factual basis for opposition. The movant shall respond to any such supplemental statement of disputed material facts as above, with its reply papers. Each statement of material facts shall be a separate document (not part of a brief) and shall not contain legal argument or conclusions of law.

Draft an opposition to this motion.

- Plaintiff's counsel (Π), oppose the defense motion addressing the causation and damages elements of your *prima facie* case.
- Defense counsel (Δ), oppose the plaintiff's motion addressing the duty and breach elements of the plaintiff's *prima facie* case.

CHAPTER 24

SEEKING SETTLEMENT AUTHORITY

Understanding the boundaries of settlement authority is an ethical expectation of an attorney. When representing a client in litigation, the topic of settlement can arise numerous times throughout the course of the litigation timeline. From the moment of intake, a matter may be faced with a settlement offer. Throughout the course of discovery, a defense attorney may present an offer to resolve the matter in lieu of continued depositions. And often, matters proceed until trial and settle just prior or because of a pre-trial settlement conference. It is therefore imperative for a litigator to understand the process of settlement and where authority lies at any given time.

Plaintiffs make demands. Defendants make offers. Typically, a defendant will not make an offer until a plaintiff makes a demand, which makes sense since the plaintiff has brought the lawsuit. A defendant will also not negotiate against himself, meaning, once a demand is made and a counteroffer is placed, there is no change to the offer until there is a change to the demand (or a conditional demand is made). This is the process of settlement. The exchange of demands and offers by those represented in litigation is of course handled by the respective attorneys.

A plaintiff's attorney must work with the client to counsel the client as to the expected value of the case. When assessing case value, both the value of the injury and the likelihood of success on liability must be considered. For instance, the value of a million-dollar injury where liability is 0 percent is not the same as a million-dollar injury. Counseling a client through the balance between liability and damages is an important part of the process and a key to successful resolution of cases via settlement. On the other hand, a defendant's attorney often works with an insurance company or self-insured entity to obtain a range within which to resolve a matter. This range of authority is what governs the value of the offer.

And where does the client fit into this process? The client holds the ultimate decision on settlement. Period. Ethically, an attorney cannot force or coerce a client to settle a matter. The decision to end pursuit of a lawsuit (or pre-suit matter) in exchange for a sum of money lies squarely in the hands of the client. So, where does the attorney come in? The attorney's role in this process is the intermediary between the opposing counsel and the client. The attorney has the dual role of negotiating with opposing counsel on the client's behalf and counseling the client on *a reasonable range* of settlements. The challenge for the attorney is keeping the client within this range of reasonable expectations and negotiating in a constructive manner with opposing counsel to maximize that range.

EXERCISE 24: Π AND Δ

As indicated in the pretrial order, the parties are scheduled to attend a settlement conference held by a magistrate judge. The parties are not required to attend the conference, but all counsel participating must have settlement authority from their respective clients in advance. Draft a letter to your client seeking that authority.

- Plaintiff's counsel (Π), draft a letter to Schott.
- Defense counsel (Δ), draft a letter to Royal.

CHAPTER 25

SETTLEMENT MEMORANDUM

A settlement memorandum is a confidential document exchanged between parties in a lawsuit (or submitted to a mediator or magistrate) outlining their position, settlement goals, and arguments for resolving the dispute without trial. These memoranda help the parties negotiate a settlement by summarizing key legal and factual points and proposing a resolution.

A settlement memorandum is not typically filed with the court and is usually prepared for a court-ordered settlement conference before a magistrate or a mediation session with a neutral third party. Some mediators or magistrates require the parties to exchange memoranda with each other, while others s require only that the parties provide a memorandum to the mediator or magistrate.

There is no standard format for a settlement memorandum, though many mediators and magistrates have their own forms or templates for litigators to follow. Unless otherwise specified, in your memorandum you should summarize: the facts; the legal issues and claims; the damages and relief sought; and the settlement negotiations to date. You may attach documentation as appropriate.

Keep your memoranda concise. Settlement memoranda are typically under ten pages. Be persuasive but professional—don't attack the opposing party. Be realistic—an unreasonable demand could thwart negotiations.

EXERCISE 25: Π AND Δ

As indicated in the pretrial order, the parties are scheduled to attend a settlement conference held by a magistrate judge. Prior to the conference, each party is directed to submit to the court a confidential memorandum addressing the following:

1. The case caption;
2. The names and email addresses of counsel to appear at the conference on behalf of the party;

3. The name of the party or the party's representative, including insurer if applicable (with title or position) who will be available to respond via telephone during the conference;
4. The status of any pending motions;
5. The status of discovery;
6. A brief statement of the elements and manner of proof of the party's claims and/or defenses;
7. A brief statement of the party's damages and manner of proof of their damages or, as appropriate, its position on damages claimed by any opposing party;
8. The last demand and/or offer;
9. Any other matters that counsel believe may be relevant to settlement discussions; and
10. The signature of counsel responsible for representations in the memorandum.

Draft this settlement memorandum.

CHAPTER 26

SETTLEMENT CONFERENCE

A settlement conference is a meeting between the parties in a lawsuit, their attorneys, and a neutral third party (typically a mediator or magistrate) to discuss resolving the case without going to trial. These conferences can be court-ordered or voluntary. Each mediator or magistrate may handle a settlement conference differently, so it can be helpful to consult with other attorneys you know who have previously appeared before that mediator or magistrate.

Often the mediator or magistrate may allow each side to make a brief statement summarizing their case. This is not a formal argument. It is simply a chance to state your position and highlight key points.

Then the mediator or magistrate will likely meet with each party separately to discuss the strengths and weaknesses of the case, the likely outcomes at trial, the risks of continuing litigation, and possible settlement terms. This is where negotiation happens, with the mediator or magistrate facilitating that negotiation.

The plaintiff typically makes an initial settlement demand. The defendant responds with a counteroffer. The parties go back and forth until an agreement is reached or it becomes clear no settlement will happen. In some cases, multiple sessions are necessary to reach a settlement or a determination that no settlement is possible.

If an agreement is reached, the terms are put in writing, and resolved claims (or the entire case) may be dismissed accordingly. If no agreement is reached, the case can proceed to trial.

EXERCISE 26: Π AND Δ

After communicating with your client, you understand the boundaries of your authority to settle. Attempt to negotiate a settlement with the assistance of the magistrate judge by engaging in a discussion.

CHAPTER 27

SETTLEMENT AGREEMENT

Settlement agreements can be reached in a variety of ways, including via counsel-to-counsel negotiations, court settlement conferences, or mediations and arbitrations. When an agreement is reached, the terms must be memorialized and executed between the parties. Doing so ensures that parties can enforce the agreement should a party not honor the agreement.

The terms of settlement agreements may vary depending on the nature of the matter, size of the settlement, and other factors which may alter the need for additional language or documentation. Generally, however, settlement agreements will include specifics as to the amount and structure of any settlement and the relinquishment of certain rights in exchange. An important part of a settlement agreement is the description of the matter that the settlement regards and the parties who are released because of the settlement payment. For once a settlement is reached and the settlement papers are executed, the matter is complete, and no further retribution can be pursued relative to the matter.

Preparing for a successful settlement agreement requires clear communication and understanding between the parties. This is of course the foundation of contracts. Once drafted, careful review is of particular importance given the finality of an executed settlement release and its effect on the parties.

EXERCISE 27: Π AND Δ

You successfully settled the dispute giving rise to litigation in this case. Draft a settlement agreement consistent with the terms of the settlement.

CHAPTER 28

NOTICE OF VOLUNTARY DISMISSAL/NOTICE TO THE COURT

The Notice of Voluntary Dismissal and corresponding notice to the court are important documents within the litigation process. Upon conclusion of any file litigated prior to trial, the parties must notify the court. Doing so not only keeps the judge apprised of the status of the matter but also allows the court to clean up active cases within the system.

Under Rule 41(a) of the Federal Rules of Civil Procedure, a Notice of Voluntary Dismissal is typically a one-page document, which following its caption and heading, notifies the court and counsel that the plaintiff and its counsel give notice that the instant matter is voluntarily dismissed. Key to this language is whether the voluntary dismissal is *with* or *without* prejudice against the defendants. A case that is dismissed "without prejudice" is temporarily dismissed, as the plaintiff is allowed to refile or bring the case elsewhere. A case that is dismissed "with prejudice" is permanently dismissed.

From the defense perspective, a notice to the court at the end of a matter comes in the form of a short letter. The letter should be addressed to the court with a copy to opposing counsel, and the caption should note the case name and number. The substance of the letter should provide clarity as to which party the drafter represents and the basis for the notice (i.e., the matter has settled).

Before preparing and filing any Notice of Voluntary Dismissal or notice to the court, it is best practice to be sure that all required paperwork in connection with any settlement has been prepared, executed, and exchanged. In short, the final step in the litigation process is finalizing these two documents.

EXERCISE 28: Π AND Δ

Because you successfully settled the case, you must now notify the court and terminate the action.

- Plaintiff's counsel (Π), draft a notice of voluntary dismissal.
- Defense counsel (Δ), draft a simple letter to the court notifying the presiding judge that the case has settled.

CHAPTER 29

CLOSING THE FILE

Recall at the beginning of an attorney-client relationship, a letter of engagement or retainer agreement is executed, outlining the responsibilities and expectations of both parties. Just as care is applied when forming an attorney-client relationship, care must be applied when ending the relationship. A client may terminate representation at any time, and an attorney may close a file or move to withdraw from a matter at any time. When one party ends the relationship, or when the representation reaches its natural end point upon conclusion of services, it is important for the attorney to properly close the file to protect the interests of both parties.

During the pre-suit phase, matters are brought in during intake for purposes of investigation. Following investigation, an assessment is made as to whether the matter is viable to continue to settlement or suit or whether the matter should be closed (i.e., no viable claims or little to no expected recovery). In this instance, it is important to advise the client of the termination of the representation, and further, it is important to advise the client that certain time limitations on various claims may exist. It is best to communicate this information both verbally and in writing. In doing so, it is best practice to remind the client that he/she may seek other counsel to provide an opinion and/or continued representation.

In litigation matters, a similar procedure is taken. Here, however, the court is involved, which adds a layer to any file closure. In the normal course of representation, upon conclusion of the case via settlement or trial, the court is made aware of the end of the representation. However, in the event an attorney moves to withdraw from the matter, court approval is required through motion procedure. If a client terminates the representation early, often a Consent to Change Attorney form is completed if new counsel is involved, or else the court is notified that the client has discontinued pursuit of the case, and the file is closed in the system.

The key here is to be sure that *all parties*, including the court if applicable, are a part of the closure process. This protects not only a client's right to pursue various claims but also protects the attorney in the process of closing a case. Matters such as the reimbursement of fee deposits, billing for completed work, retention of client file, and potential statutes of limitations should be addressed.

EXERCISE 29: Π AND Δ

With the settlement of this case, representation of your client has concluded. Draft a closure letter to your client as well as a memo to the file documenting the closure of the case and your efforts to comply with any retention policies and ethical requirements.

- Plaintiff's counsel (Π), direct your letter to Schott.
- Defense counsel (Δ), direct your letter to Royal.

PART IV

CONCLUSION

Congratulations, you have now officially litigated a realistic civil case from start to conclusion. Along the way, you developed a series of portable skills. Although this case happened to involve a tort, those skills are equally applicable no matter what the underlying subject area of a case happens to be.

In practice, each case is unique. You may spend more or less time in each phase of litigation. You may engage in steps of the process that weren't covered in this book. Regardless, if you worked diligently through the exercises, you should feel more prepared for practice than you were before you began using this book. In addition, the skills practiced should better prepare you for the NextGen bar exam.

You now have a working understanding of the litigation process and the skills to be an effective litigator. Using this book was challenging, but you will be a better lawyer for your efforts.

INDEX

Principal materials are indicated by italics.